CW01500896

JUST KEEP GOING!

A Cape Wrath Trail Odyssey

Will Cove

DEDICATION

To all the people who supported me with donations to my nominated charity, Mind. Together we raised over £1000. Thank you.

To my long-suffering family, Jo, Mia and Florence, for letting me go and allowing me to come back.

THANKS

Many thanks to Dawn Leggott, a good friend, who proofread this account, turning my ramblings into a coherent script.

CONTENTS

THE ROUTE

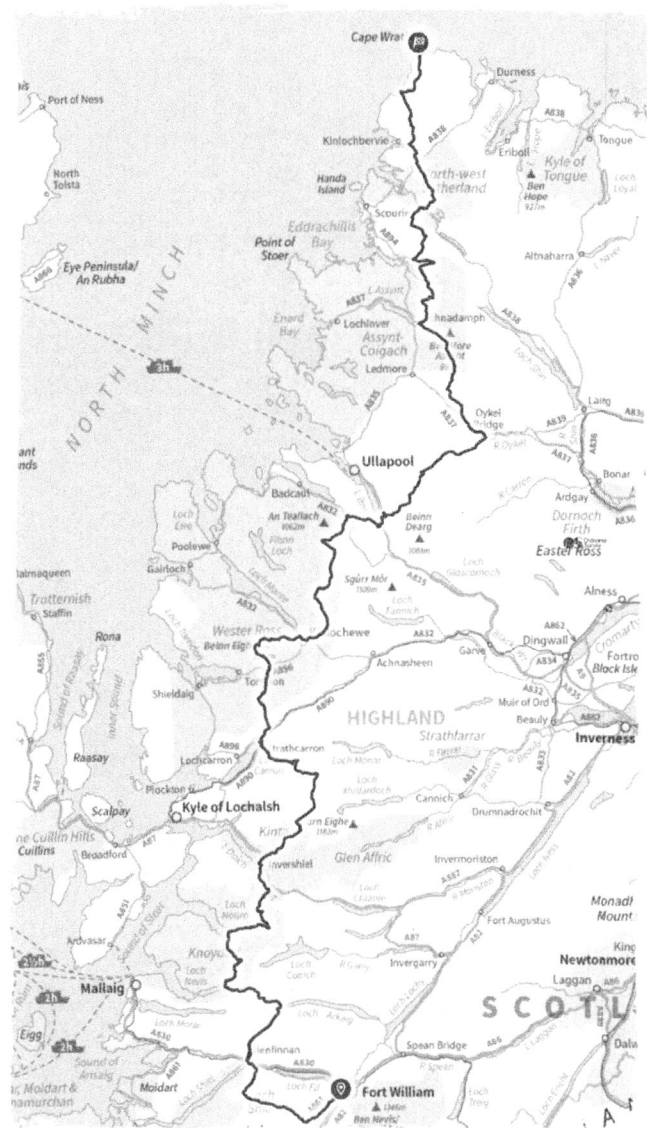

INTRODUCTION

The Cape Wrath Trail (Cape Wrath Trail) is the world's finest and toughest long distance walk that no one has ever heard of. Deceivingly, it is not a trail, but a route, running the length of the Scottish Highlands from Fort William to the most northwestern point of mainland Britain, Cape Wrath. Over 240 miles, passing through magnificent untamed vast empty landscapes. Doing this trail involves crossing the boggy and boulder-strewn back country of northwest Scotland – one of the last wild areas of the British Isles – with no signposts and often without any paths whatsoever. It is supposed to take between two and three weeks to walk it, although someone has run it in under five days. Apparently the trail should only be undertaken by experienced walkers who have honed their walking, navigation and outdoors skills, and are very comfortable with being outside in harsh conditions. How hard can it be? What could possibly go wrong?

Oh, and just to be clear, I am not doing this stroll as part of a guided group. Oh no. I am doing it by myself, alone. Carrying my own food, my own shelter, my own maps, my own compass. Under my own steam, one foot in front of the other. Self guided and maybe self deluded.

Why am I doing this challenge for charity? Why am

I raising money and awareness for Mind? These are good questions, but the question that occurred to me is: "If I was going to do this walk, why not try and collect a few pennies for a good cause at the same time?"

Why Mind? I'm not sure why I'm drawn to raising funds for a mental health charity. Perhaps it's because I feel mental health is often unseen, overlooked and swept under the carpet. Perhaps it's because I feel mental health charities tend to be the poor relation to the physical health charities. Perhaps it's because maybe I am a little unhinged myself in attempting this Cape Wrath Trail challenge. As an aside, I also like their squiggly logo and apparently, according to the internet, it will make me feel good to raise money for charity… so it seems to be a win-win strategy!

My target? Well, this is an arbitrary number, but I thought I would aim for £500. There is a reason for this figure. It will take me (according to Google) approximately 500,000 steps – yes, that's half a million times of putting one foot in front of the other – to complete this jaunt. So that's a mere 0.1p for every step I take. It doesn't sound like very much but I hope it will all add up.

The above is the blurb I put on my JustGiving page. Perhaps a little overhyped? When I wrote it, I didn't really know what I was getting into. I decided that a bit of hype never hurt anybody…

CAPE WRATH TRIAL…

**The Cape Wrath Fail… The Cape Wrath Fantasy…
The Cape Wrath whatever…**

At this stage, three months before kickoff, it was more the
Cape Wrath Trial than the Cape Wrath Trail. Or maybe the
Cape Wrath Obsession or the Cape Wrath White Elephant.
Take your pick. I had not even heard of this walk a year
ago and now its shadow was cast over each day and there
were still over 90 days to go before I started it. I suspect
I'd allowed the Cape Wrath Trail mystique to get the better
of me.

When a walk is quietly hailed as possibly "The world's
finest and toughest walk that no one has ever heard of", it
kind of has a hypnotic aura to it. The long distance walking
sirens clear their collective throats and belt out, "This is it!
Come get me!"

OK, so I've done a couple of strolls. Self propelled
across rugged land. Carrying my own supplies and shelter.
I kind of enjoyed it. I enjoyed it a lot. There were parts
I loved and there were parts that weren't so good. If
I'm totally honest, there were parts that I'd rather never
experience again, ever. But, also if I'm totally honest, the
sum of the bad and good parts of previous wanderings
always resulted in an enormous surplus of well-being.

5

So far I have learned many lessons. I have been cold and hungry. I have experienced kindness and generosity from strangers. I have been awed by natural wonders and inspiring views. I have no regrets. Best foot forward and all that.

PREPARATION, PREPARATION, PREPARATION...

Maps, guidebooks and research

There's nothing like planning a long distance walk to fill the long dark winter nights preceding embarkation. For Wainwright's Coast to Coast walk I was able to buy an OS strip map at 1:25k scale in a booklet format where each open spread perfectly fitted my Ortlieb map case. There was also a wealth of information about supplies and facilities along the route, all freely available on the internet. How I wish all long distance walks could be that simple. For my Southern Upland Way walk I painstakingly took screen grabs from Bing maps OS overlay, again at 1:25k scale, and carefully stitched them together in Photoshop to make my own strip map. It took a while, and because the Southern Upland Way was a clearly way marked official trail on the ground, it all worked out very well. This time round, the Cape Wrath Trail offered no 1:25k OS strip map. There is a 1:40k strip map by Harvey, which I bought, but I like, and am very familiar with, the OS 1:25k maps. The Cape Wrath Trail is not a waymarked trail. There are no signposts, and there are not many pubs and shops along the route, or actually much civilisation at all for that matter, so getting lost and finding help is not really an option. It appeared to be a much more serious proposition.

Eventually I decided to purchase all of the OS 1:25k maps that covered the entire route. Twelve of them in total. I wasn't about a haul 12 OS maps along the trail so I carefully marked my route on them with a yellow highlighter pen and then, over a quiet Saturday, scanned all the relevant sections and stitched the images together in Photoshop. I also bought the Cicerone guide to the Cape Wrath Trail by Iain Harper, which I read from cover to cover, twice. Due to my goldfish capacity to retain information, and because I didn't want to carry it (all extra weight), I also scanned that in, and stitched it onto the dead spaces of my self-made strip map. Since the summer of 2018, when I committed myself mentally to the Cape Wrath Trail, I had filled much of my work and evening downtime by reading Cape Wrath Trail blogs and watching Cape Wrath Trail YouTube video diaries (much to the despair and ridicule of my wife!). There is a wealth of information out there if you are prepared to dig. I wholeheartedly thank all those people who were prepared to share their experiences. And so, to finish off my personalised route map, I added the shops, hotels, B&Bs, wild camp spots, river crossings, tricky sections and any other information I had gleaned from the blogs I had read.

I had created a highly personalised and highly detailed document that fitted neatly onto 44 sheets measuring 28cm square. Each was custom made to fit into my Ortlieb map case. Previous walks have shown me that I can cover, on average, three of these squares in a day. I expected this stroll to be a wee bit more challenging. So 44 sheets divided by two and a half equals 18; that's 18 days of walking. Having worked out what I thought was a pretty relaxed schedule, I hoped to be in Durness by day 19. This wasn't going to break any records and I hoped it wouldn't break my spirit or push me too far beyond my comfort zone. I hoped to do it more swiftly, however. My schedule didn't include any rest days (I'm hopeless at sitting still) and perhaps more importantly it didn't allow for foul weather intervening.

Kit

Oh, the wonder of the world's latest high-tech kit. It is very easy to become obsessed with it. I constantly reminded myself that homo sapiens, as hunter gatherers, traversed the Earth through ice ages tens to hundreds of thousands of years before I was around. They were dressed in little more than animal hides, not a sniff of Gore-Tex, and they survived, as we are all living proof of it. Ok, so they might not have had a great life expectancy and they probably lived harsh and gruelling lives but, nevertheless, something like the Cape Wrath Trail was probably a morning stroll for them.

I look back now at my first foray into long distance walking. I had walked 40 miles. Back then that distance seemed a ridiculously long way to me. I set out with a borrowed backpack and a borrowed sleeping bag, though I had invested the princely sum of £20 in a tent. I walked from my house on the outskirts of Barnsley to Edale in the Peak District. It was a mild August bank holiday weekend.

I understand now that those first steps into the unknown probably took more courage than the epic walking adventures I have done since. I learned a great deal on that first walk, about kit, about food, about way finding, about the weather, about my body, but most of all I learned how liberating and satisfying travelling under my own steam can be.

I have now honed my kit through the experiences of two previous proper walks – Wainwright's Coast to Coast and the Southern Upland Way. That first walk to Edale taught me that the lightweight backpacker's holy trinity is the backpack, tent and sleeping bag. Next to the food I carried, those three items made up the bulk of the weight. I swiftly realised that a £20 tent wasn't going to keep me dry and, weighing several kilos, it was also quite heavy. I realised that the borrowed sleeping bag, which also weighed several kilos, wasn't going to keep me warm even on a mild summer's night. And the borrowed backpack, adding a couple more kilos, left my back and shoulders sore and aching. Those early homo sapiens may well have walked thousands of miles in animal skins but I am sure they were much tougher than me. After significant research, I took a very deep breath, and bought a Terra Nova Laser Competition tent, a Sea to Summit Spark II sleeping bag and an Osprey Exos 38 litre backpack. At a single stroke I had knocked the holy trinity combined weight from well over 6kg down to under 2kg. My bank balance was also much lighter. With a few years and more than a thousand miles under my boots I feel this was a good investment. If I could time travel and advise my younger self, I would suggest spending even more money and invest in the warmer Sea to Summit Spark III or IV sleeping bag and so avoid the odd chilly night in particularly icy conditions. As for the tent and backpack, they have been, and continue to be, excellent value for money.

Given my previous long distance walking experiences, for this walk my kit preparation really just involved fine tuning rather than anything new and groundbreaking. I had my 50th birthday a few months before I planned to set off, and friends and family were asking what I would like for a present. Now, I hadn't arrived at the half-century mark without pretty much acquiring all the "stuff" I was ever likely to need and then some extra bits just to be sure. I really didn't need anything else but suspected that I may well end up with a dozen giant scented candles by accident if I didn't offer my well-intentioned family and friends some guidance. This definitely comes under the category of a First World problem. As mentioned, I felt I could do with more warmth at night, but buying another sleeping bag seemed wrong when I already owned a pretty good one. I decided that a more pragmatic and flexible solution would be to purchase a new down jacket to sleep in and keep me snug and warm through sub-zero nights. There was one that looked awesome, but due to cost constraints was, for me, out of reach. The Rab Infinity G down jacket. Probably the best warmth to weight ratio garment money can buy. Thanks to the generosity of my friends and family I became the proud owner of this gold-plated goose down feather jacket. It hung in my wardrobe for months unworn. I had high hopes of cosy nights in the Scottish Highlands.

Another significant kit upgrade/purchase was the Therm-a-Rest Neo Air three-quarter length inflatable sleeping mat and pillow. I had used three-quarter length self-inflating sleeping mats, which had served me well, but decided that for a moderate outlay I could save several hundred grams plus pack volume. I tested the Neo Air on a local weekend two-night jaunt in the Peak District and a slightly further flung mini-adventure to the Lake District, with positive results. When combined with the Therm-a-Rest pump sack, which doubles as my backpack's waterproof liner, inflating the air bed was a cinch. I feel this upgrade represents a relatively small weight gain to expenditure ratio, which means I should be giving myself a firm metaphorical slap round the face and reminding myself that I may be on the verge of following the "all the gear, no idea" Pied Piper down the rabbit hole.

Wet feet or dry feet?

There appeared to be two strategies with regards to footwear for this walk and walking on wet terrain in general. There's the traditional Gore-Tex lined waterproof walking boot option and then there's the lightweight trail shoe approach. Both have their advantages and disadvantages. The benefits of wearing walking boots is that your feet will stay dry for longer so will be less likely to suffer from blisters, and walking boots have good ankle support. The downside of walking boots is that their waterproof integrity will eventually be breached, either over the top of the ankles or because their waterproof membrane fails, and then they take a long time to dry out. Trail shoes offer no defence against water but will dry quickly on the go and what they lack in ankle support can be made up for through the use of walking poles. The disadvantage of trail shoes is that wet feet will possibly result in blistering and trench foot. I've got to admit that I have always worn walking boots on my previous long distance walks and the idea of walking with feet that are any wetter than they need to be seemed an anathema to me. I had read a number of blogs that suggested I was fooling myself if I thought I could keep my feet dry whilst walking the Cape Wrath Trail and indicated that I should embrace the dark side. So my solution? I set off in walking boots and carried a pair of Innov8 Talon running shoes in my backpack for the river crossings. If it transpired that I was comfortable walking with wet feet then I would post the boots home and embrace the wet feet revolution...

River crossings

Of all the potential challenges that lay ahead of me on the Cape Wrath Trail, it was the thought of the river crossings that kept me awake at night. I was comfortable with long periods of solitude and with being far from home and creature comforts. I was even at ease with the time and distance this madcap escapade would involve. It was the potentially dangerous river crossings that gave me nightmares. I had read about river fording techniques and even put the theories to the test in my local streams after heavy rainfall. I had been reminded of how even shallow water, not even knee height, in a fast flowing water course, can make it very difficult for me to maintain a secure balance.

This element of the walk was very much in the lap of the Gods. How much it rained and when it rained was out of my control. All I could do was prepare myself and

my kit/strategy for river crossings. There seemed to be
a consensus on how to cross a river. Firstly, and if at all
possible, without doubt the best way of crossing a river is,
and always will be, to use a well-built bridge. Failing that,
a common sense approach seems to me to be: 1. Gauge
depth and flow; 2. If depth and flow seem reasonable,
proceed; 3. Traverse diagonally across/upstream into the
current; 4. Use walking poles for stability. And that was it.

I also came across several strategies for footwear for
river crossings. There was the wade on in there laissez-faire
approach and put up with wet boots and feet. There was
the alternative footwear for river crossings strategy, varying
from trail shoes to beach shoes made from neoprene with
rubber soles. And then there was the inventive method
of using heavy-duty rubble sacks and Velcro straps to
keep them in place to make super lightweight waders. My
conclusions were that I am not happy with walking in
drenched boots for days on end, and although the rubble
sack method was very effective, I found it wasn't a long-
term option, as they soon developed holes and leaked. This
left me with the alternative footwear approach. I narrowed
this down further to the beach shoes versus the trail shoes.
A pair of Innov8 Talon trainers weighed in pretty much the
same as the beach shoes but were much more versatile, i.e.
they were actually a potential substitute for walking boots
in the country I was crossing. So trail shoes it was.

Training…

I had done a bit of "training" through January in a
haphazard way. This mainly consisted of cycling a 25-mile

loop and walking another 10-mile loop, sometimes both on the same day. I did not have a strategic approach. I just figured that a half-hearted fitness level would be a bonus, and anything beyond that would be a plus. Besides, I've always felt that the first few days of any long distance walk was the natural training period.

I do not consider myself a natural cyclist but found it was an efficient method of increasing my fitness. Where I live is not exactly level country but that's all for the better. I don't ride a sleek mile-munching road bike; I ride a solid, chunky mountain bike, complete with a heavy bike lock and water bottle. I'm not racing against other folk on Strava; I'm up against myself, so it didn't matter. Despite not associating myself with being a cyclist, I found that I enjoyed the solitary hours battling rain and wind on endless tarmac, and have observed that it's not that different from covering endless miles on foot. Occasionally I cycled plugged in to music, mostly fairly intense dance tunes. The time passed more swiftly.

On foot I had been taking ten litres of water for a stroll, filling my backpack with old milk bottles brimming with ballast. Over 12kg on my back. My wife chuckled each time I took my "water" for a walk, and I don't blame her, as it did seem ridiculous. I was a tad self-conscious on exiting the front door, Gore-Tex clad, walking poles in hand, complete with a pack. Fortunately within minutes I'd be out of sight and striding anonymously through farmland.

To share or not to share

I have always enjoyed walking by myself. I've enjoyed

the solace, the time to think – so much time to think. It is extreme meditation. I've got to know myself very well. Apparently many people pay good money for a mindful meditation yoga retreat for a week or two, but I wholeheartedly recommend just going for a long walk. You can't beat it.

My previous walks have been solo events. And wonderful for it. I'm not a complete introvert. Walking by yourself opens you up to meeting people and as a result I have made new friends. Encounters with complete strangers who have a shared life philosophy often lead to a great night's craic and kinship.

When a friend suggested that he would like to join me for part of the walk, I've got to admit that I was in two minds (my humble apologies Steve!). It wasn't my style. Not the way I roll. Not the way I stroll. It would be a very different experience. But after much thought and pondering, I realised that because it would be different it might even be better. He was only proposing to join me for the last few days, so I figured that after a week or two of blundering through Scottish bogs by myself, I might actually enjoy the companionship of a friend. The whole plan was hopelessly up in the air though, as my schedule was at best tenuous and very much at the mercy of the weather. I reckoned it would be a minor miracle if the end of my walk actually coincided with the time Steve had booked holiday off work. As it happened, my friend sustained an injury during his rather rigorous training and decided it would be foolhardy for him to go through with it.

My brother-in-law, David, also suggested that he meet

up with me. His idea was to meet me at the end of the walk, at the Cape Wrath lighthouse. That was until he realised that you couldn't drive there and that he would need to take a small open-top fishing boat/ferry, fine weather permitting, and then a ten-mile minibus drive along a rough track to get to the lighthouse. Not deterred, David said he would meet me, if not actually at Cape Wrath, then at Durness, which is the nearest village connected to the regular UK road network. This would be a huge bonus for me as it would negate the lengthy and expensive process of getting myself home to West Yorkshire. There was still the slight niggling detail of my topsy-turvy schedule aligning with his holiday leave. Stranger things have happened and I am eternally an optimist.

4 weeks to go...

I set up a JustGiving page and to my amazement within a few days I had raised £314.99 for Mind, my nominated charity, and I hadn't even set off! The JustGiving site sent me prompts each week to update my supporters who, although very generous, numbered fewer than ten. What could I tell them? What was there to tell them? That my training, by then, had deteriorated to commuting to work by bike? Twelve miles each way. There was no walking involved. It struck me that it was the equivalent to swimming lengths in preparation to run a marathon. I was feeling a little nervous and slightly terrified but I would have been worried if I had been feeling any other way. It's got to be the natural response to stepping out into the unknown.

I was going to take a low-tech approach to this stroll. Maps and compass. No GPS. No satellite tracker. No SOS beacon. I figured that, short of a cataclysmic cosmic event (and then I'd have bigger but short-lived worries), the sun would always rise in the east and set in the west, and I knew that the route was mostly in a northerly direction. It all seemed pretty straightforward. However, beyond getting hopelessly lost (and historically I've always managed to get myself un-lost, eventually), there was a nagging worry, which I had done my best to put out of my mind… what would happen if something went wrong? If I suffered catastrophic equipment failure? Snapped an ankle? Was trapped by raging rivers? As a general life rule I've tried to take responsibility for my actions. I try not to worry about stuff that's beyond my control and minimise the risks where I can. But I couldn't ignore that much of the terrain I'd be passing through has little to no mobile phone coverage. A relatively minor mishap could potentially become life threatening. I already felt a wee bit guilty deserting my family for three weeks, and I'd feel really bad putting them through the stress and worry of me disappearing altogether. So despite my reckless tendencies and against my thrifty Yorkshire judgement (definition of a Yorkshire man: a Scotsman with all the generosity squeezed out of them), I looked into hiring or buying a satellite tracker. I soon learned that these toys cost £200 to hire and £400 to buy (plus a monthly subscription). You may consider this a cheap and worthwhile investment as insurance against your untimely demise, but from where I was sitting (jaw agape at my computer keyboard after a bit of Googling), it all struck me as a bit expensive for a few weeks' walking… clearly I see my life as cheap. Ever resourceful, I thought I'd put a shoutout on Facebook:

"Does anyone have a tracker I could borrow? Please? Pretty please?"

And then a minor miracle happened. A friend, Neil, contacted me and agreed to let me borrow his tracker. It was a practically brand new Garmin InReach Explorer with all the bells and whistles, and apparently I could even send text messages to loved ones (but fortunately not update my Facebook status). He had bought it for a paragliding trip in Morocco a month before. A trip he had safely returned from. As it isn't considered an essential or necessary bit of flying kit in England, he generously let me look after it for a few weeks. So now I could potentially be followed across Scotland via a web page. Just like the Red Bull X-Alps*, except it's a much shorter distance, I wasn't crossing the Alps, there was no flying involved and it wasn't a race. Also, I was not sponsored by Red Bull. The Cape Wrath Trail does feature on their website though, even though I'd never consider walking to be an extreme sport. But apart from all that it was just like the Red Bull X-Alps…

I just had to work out how to use the darn thing…

*The Red Bull X-Alps is billed as the world's toughest adventure race, in which competitors must hike or fly (using a paraglider) over 1000 kilometres across the Alps.

Fundraising

I was surprised, nope, I was amazed, at how supportive friends and family were of me doing this adventure. And how much they had donated to my nominated charity, Mind. I was a tad blown away.

I have a small confession to make. I was going to walk

this walk regardless of doing some greater good of raising funds for a worthy cause. I had done walks before, perhaps not quite of this magnitude, but nevertheless they probably would have been regarded as fair achievements. And it had never crossed my mind to raise money for charity. I'd always regarded them as selfish endeavours.

The fundraising seed had been sown and germinated during a meal at my local Indian Restaurant, the Palace Tandori in Denby Dale. It had been the evening of my 50th birthday, a Wednesday night in November. A local low-key celebration with a handful of good friends and family. The Cape Wrath Trail walk had already solidified as my next challenge and the point was raised, perhaps by me after several glasses of wine, that it would be a good opportunity to do some fundraising for a good cause.

My natural tendency has been to shy away from fundraising for a few reasons. The first – perhaps the main – reason, and the weakest reason, is that I am a fairly private person. I have no desire to tell my friends, let alone the world, what I'm doing. Secondly, I'm surrounded by people doing mud runs, 5k's, 10k's, half marathons, marathons, triathlons, ironmans, one peak, two peaks, three peaks, egg and spoon races, ice bucket challenges, sofa challenges(?!?) and on and on and on. All cracking goals (except maybe for the sofa challenge) and good luck to them, but I had a niggling suspicion that it had all become a little too commercialised. And maybe it had, but what I have learned is that those who feel that way need not participate (thank you for the pep talk, Julie). And lastly, probably the worst reason that I didn't publicise what I do is the elephant in the room, the boogie man in my closet... what if I fail? Quietly ducking out under the public radar because of injury/bad weather/equipment failure is easy. Bailing mid task once I have committed and broadcast my intentions to the world is another matter. This subsequently increases pressure on me to succeed but I reasoned that it was all inside my head. Not succeeding through injury, bad weather or equipment failure would or wouldn't happen regardless of whether I had publicised my intentions. However, everyone would get to know if I failed. Sooo... there may well be some validity to keeping outlandish adventures under my hat.

2 weeks to go…

Food glorious food… On previous walks I had come up with some solid winners on the menu front. In fact, so good that I had ended up eating the same thing for days on end, which inevitably became my favourite dish's downfall. I discovered that despite being heartening, tasty and filling, there is only so much mac cheese and chorizo my palette can endure. My go-to breakfast warming starter to the day of Ready Brek and golden syrup also became a little jaded over time. With the echoes of food repetitious tedium from my stroll a year ago, I vowed to explore and increase my culinary repertoire. There existed the prerequisite that the meal had to be light (aka dehydrated), easy to cook in one small pot and swift to prepare, as I might well be tired after a day's walking. Over the past few months I had been buying various random foodstuffs, some on a whim and some based on ideas gleaned from research. One Sunday I cooked up and sampled my bounty. The contenders were (drum roll ... dry ice ... lasers...) powdered mash, Ainsley's pilau rice, bean feast spaghetti bolognese, and some lentil and bacon Cup a Soup which had been on special offer. First up was the lentil and bacon Cup a Soup, which was a complete fail. It vaguely resembled a warm, wet version of smoky bacon crisps. Fortunately my youngest daughter declared it delicious and snaffled the barely touched mug that I had brewed. Next up was the powdered mash, and my hopes weren't high. To try and improve their chances, I mixed it with powdered milk, butter, dehydrated onions and some random Polish seasoning which, from the ingredients on the packet, appeared to be mostly salt and colouring. It took no time to prepare – just add boiling water – but the result looked like baby sick. In the interests of furthering my research and benefiting human knowledge, I forced myself to try it. It actually tasted pretty good. I could barely believe my taste buds. This was the first time in my life that I have eaten powdered mash and the darn stuff did not taste a million miles off the real McCoy. And by adding the butter, onions and seasoning, the overall result was elevated to well beyond my expectations. I reckoned it would be a perfect match to wild haggis. Now I just had to work out how to hunt a haggis and my dietary needs would be sorted. Ainsley Harriott's pilau rice mix took a reasonable five minutes to cook and was also very acceptable. That left the bean feast bolognese. Surprisingly, at least to me, I felt this was the greatest success of all my food experimenting. It tasted great and almost indistinguishable from its meaty counterpart. I accept I may be exaggerating, but I reckoned that at the end of a tough day in the wind-swept Highlands, my expectations would be fairly low. The bean feast's one downside was that it took 20 minutes to cook. Not that long when you are at home in your cosy kitchen, but in the aforementioned wind-swept Highlands with limited supplies of fuel, cooking time was a consideration. Nevertheless, I decided its flavour and heartiness outweighed its extravagant preparation time. I was set. I now had four meals I could rotate. Oh, and on the breakfast front, I couldn't think of improving the clear winning formula of my pre-prepared Ready Brek mix except to add raisins and peanut butter. All I can say is that you shouldn't knock it until you've tried it. As Oscar Wilde said, try anything once, except incest and Morris dancing…

I also phoned up three places I had identified as locations I could send resupply parcels to. The first drew a blank. Well, not exactly a blank but they were only prepared to accept my parcel if I booked a £100 room. As this project's schedule was so weather dependent, I was not confident that I would be where I wanted to be on any particular week, let alone day, so I declined their offer. The next place claimed they had been advised by their insurance company not to take parcels unless customers made a booking. I had no idea that some remote Scottish hostelry might be a terrorist target. However, they were happy to take a £20 booking for a bed in their bunk barn which could be upgraded to one of their hotel rooms if one was available, and they were flexible on my arrival date. Clearly, their insurance company didn't think terrorists' budgets stretched beyond £20. The last of my three preliminary choices didn't bat an eyelid and weren't particularly worried about the day I got there or if I stayed the night or not. Now that's true Scottish hospitality. I phoned a couple more places on my plan B list. Both had no objections and were very friendly. Resupply points now sorted, I just had to make up the parcels.

Keeping the parcels under 2kg kept the postage under £4 (small parcel). Anything over 2kg and postage costs escalated to double figures. I also decided not to post gas cartridges. Technically it is illegal, although it had worked for me in the past. This time round, because I had phoned up various places and asked what they had on the supplies front, I knew I could buy gas at Shiel Bridge and Kinlochewe.

2 days to go...

In the evening I packed my backpack, carefully checking everything against a list I had made, fully conscious that forgetting something vital could jeopardise the whole trip. And almost everything I was taking was vital. Just one of everything to save weight, no backups. Except for a compass. It was the only thing I doubled up on. I figured that if anything failed I could keep going for at least a day or two however uncomfortable I'd be. But I also reasoned that if I did not know where I was going, then the ability to keep going would become inconsequential.

This was the first time I had packed my bag with everything that I would be taking including food. I hoped it would all fit into my trusty 38 litre backpack. Perhaps it would have been wiser to have done a dry run several weeks earlier to ensure I didn't get a nasty shock and discover I only had room for half the stuff I needed. Fortunately, with careful packing, it all went in. Unfortunately, it weighed in at 14.5kg. This was significantly over my preferred maximum weight of 12kg. I reasoned that I was carrying 4 days' food (including the luxury of wine and brandy!). The weight would drop quickly enough.

1 day to go...

I had planned to work half a day to give me and my family time to drive up to Fort William in the afternoon. As with all best laid plans external influences contrived to thwart me. During my work week I had been busy preparing for a pitch. It meant a great deal for the company I was working for. Significant potential new business. That morning at work coincided with an ever-diminishing deadline. When 1pm came, I upped and left. I did feel momentarily guilty at my lack of commitment. Not for abandoning the project, as I had given it my all, but for landing the responsibility of completing the pitch on my colleagues[1]. As Douglas Adams had once said: "I love deadlines. I love the whooshing noise they make as they go by."

I had other fish to fry. I hurtled homeward, shed work clothes and donned what I would be wearing for my indefinite future. Fortunately the Cove camper van had been prepared and we were soon travelling north – the direction I'd be travelling for the next few weeks self propelled under my own steam, but for the moment I was using the relatively new invention of the internal combustion engine.

Several hours later we had been making good progress, especially considering it was the day before the Easter Bank Holiday weekend, but then the inevitable happened just south of Glasgow. The marvel that is Sat Nav suggested

1. Two weeks later when I returned to work I discovered that whilst my colleagues had completed and delivered the pitch on time, the Client Services Team had not presented the work because they were umming and erring over semantics.

we would save time with a diversion. We were rerouted away from the usual road up by Loch Lomond and into new territory via Stirling. I had recced a potential dinner stop somewhere north of Glasgow but we were now off the map. Fortunately we passed through a town large enough to have a fish and chip shop. Even more fortunately it claimed to be the best fish and chip shop in all of Scotland. I'm not sure how legitimate its bragging rights were but I can tell you it did an excellent fish supper. Suitably sated we headed onward to our wild camp destination, a Forestry Commission car park which I had scoped out earlier on the internet. Just after dusk, we wearily set up for the night and were soon bedded down.

My brother-in-law, David, sent me a "Good luck" text message. During the build-up to setting off I confided in him that I had become quite apprehensive about what I was letting myself in for and my slim chances of succeeding. However, that evening I felt very calm. I replied saying that I was no longer afraid and that arriving in the Highlands felt like I had arrived home.

DAY 1

Fort William to a few miles before Glenfinnan

Weather: Hot! A gentle wind

17 miles

649 metres of ascent

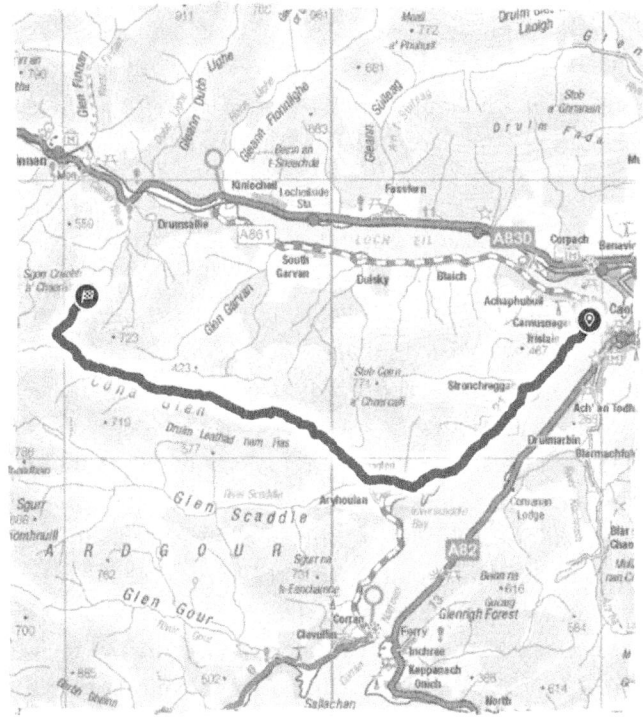

An information board in the car park promised us red squirrels. We didn't see any of the cute wee red-haired tree-dwelling critters but our wake up alarm call was courtesy of a woodpecker tapping away at a nearby trunk at 7.30am. Right on time. I couldn't have orchestrated the wildlife better if I had had the powers of Dr Dolittle.

After rousing the girls and feeding them breakfast, we emerged from the van to explore our surroundings. This is always quite exciting when we had arrived late the previous night in darkness and were unsure of what we would find. Florence observed some early arrivals at the car park bedecked in hiking gear heading out for a day. She was amazed. She couldn't quite grasp that people walked through their own volition. I think, until that moment, she believed that her dad was a lone freak who happened to be obsessed with walking and that anyone else out there had been forced or coerced into it. Much like herself.

After a quick jaunt around a forest trail, hunting the elusive woodpecker (never did spy him), we packed up and drove the last few miles to Fort William. We'd phoned the ferry operators the day before to check that there were crossings to Camusnagaul, the village across the sea loch and the start of the Cape Wrath Trail. They had assured us there were sailings; however, they were not departing from their usual place but from the West End car park. "Good thing we checked," I thought. Loch Linnhe, the sea loch that Fort William is on the shore of, was as calm as the proverbial mill pond. I asked the ferry deckhand how the weather had been this year. He told me that whilst it had been relatively dry, it had been very windy, and such a smooth crossing was rare. The young ship dog appeared very relaxed and took to chewing various passengers' luggage.

After a sedate 20 minutes, the ferry arrived at Camusnagaul, on the far side of the loch. The deckhand lowered the boat's bow ramp for a Normandy-esque beach landing. We trundled off, making sure Jo and the girls wouldn't be left behind upon the ferry's return. Last photos were snapped, hugs were exchanged, and farewells bidden. I'm not one for long drawn-out goodbyes and my mind was firmly on what lay ahead of me, so without much more ceremony I headed down the road.

The first seven miles of the Cape Wrath Trail headed southwest, doggedly away from Cape Wrath, along the A861. Fortunately the A861 is a relatively quiet road, and probably no more than a dozen cars passed me. It was a glorious day in Scotland, with horizon to horizon blue sky, which meant I was carrying my waterproofs, gaiters and fleece, thus adding another kilo to an already heavy pack. The weight was noticeable but I didn't grumble too much, as walking in sunshine was something of a novelty for me.

On the ferry there had been two cyclists and another walker. The cyclists soon overtook me and the other walker, an earnest young man clutching a Cape Wrath Trail map despite the seven miles of road walking ahead, also caught me up. We exchanged a few pleasantries and established we were both on the Cape Wrath Trail. He introduced himself as Joe, originally from Tadcaster, so a fellow Yorkshire man, but now living in London. He proudly announced that he worked as a headhunter. With a little too much disdain, I wondered how well a purveyor of human souls slept at night. I further suggested that there was a special place in Hell reserved for him right next to the bankers and the lawyers. My comments were tongue in cheek, but it was clear we had little in common. Not surprisingly, our conversation dried up and his pace outstripped mine, so I opted to stop to make a tea whilst he power walked on. Not much further along the road I passed the first of the cyclists who had suffered a catastrophic blowout and was slowly wheeling his wounded steed back to Fort William for repairs. A little further up the road I passed the second cyclist, who had stopped for refreshments, and I began to wonder whether bicycles were really an efficient means of transportation in this neck of the woods.

It was a beautiful day, better than I could have ever hoped for, but I had an underlying low-level niggling concern at the back of my thoughts. To me, walking this kind of distance is too much to comprehend. I didn't dare to begin to imagine getting to the end, especially at this early stage. Had I packed everything? Would my legs, knees and feet take the pace? Would the weather hold out? On that sunny Good Friday morning I placed my chances of getting to goal optimistically at 50%.

At the turn-off from the road that led up Cona Glen, I stopped for my second brew of the day. This marked the place where I departed from civilisation and it was my first proper foray into the Highland wilds. I lazily lowered my pack to the ground and my reading glasses fell from where I had sloppily stashed them, in an unzipped pocket, onto the grass. I couldn't believe I had been so careless. I also couldn't believe that I had been so lucky that they had not escaped whilst walking for the past couple of hours. How would have I been able to read maps without those glasses and continue this walk? I silently berated myself for my carelessness and gave thanks to any gods listening. Whilst sipping my tea and munching a Snickers I re-evaluated my chances of getting to goal down to 30%.

The heat of the afternoon sun was matched by the magnificent scenery I was now strolling through. The pathfinding was easy, just head straight up the glen following the Cona River flanked by hills on either side. The going under foot was easy, on what I would call a four-wheel drive track. It was a rough and rocky unpaved course used by farmers, gamekeepers and deer stalkers. Little did I know, but these kinds of tracks covered much of the Highlands. I caught up with Joe who had stopped for lunch and taken a dip to cool off. After brief pleasantries I headed on. A mile up the glen I found a lovely spot for lunch and went as far as soaking my feet in the icy river water.

Joe soon came by and provided me with some brief entertainment crossing a wire bridge over the river and back again. A bridge was marked on the OS map but this was the first time I had come across a wire bridge. It consisted of three wires. One to walk on and one wire each side at waist height as hand rails. The wires were quite bouncy. I instantly made up my mind that yes, theoretically, it was a potential bridge but also that it was the kind of bridge that featured in Indiana Jones films and probably the kind of bridge you would only use when there was no other option.

Fortunately, because of the dry conditions leading up to me setting off, the ground was only slightly moist and the rivers were low. Considering the Scottish Highlands' reputation I had been amazed at how little rain there had been. I had been obsessively tracking the BBC 14-day weather forecast before my departure. Forecasting is generally witchcraft and guesswork, especially in this neck of the woods, but the BBC appeared to get the on-the-day weather correct, when predicted 14 days in advance, at least half the time. Probably more by luck than judgement. I was convinced that I should have set off two weeks earlier, as I was sure the run of mild dry weather would break at any moment.

Apart from my custom-made 1:25k OS strip map complete with trail notes from Iain Harper's guide, I was using the ViewRanger app on my phone. I had very little experience of the app except for one disastrous walk in the Lake District the previous summer. It had been the August bank holiday and I specifically wanted to test bits and bobs of kit including ViewRanger. I had hastily downloaded the app and signed up for the seven-day free trial. I also thought I had downloaded the maps for offline use. I had worked out a circular route starting at Helwith Bridge, up and around to Scafell Pike, onto the Old Man of Coniston and then looping back round to the starting point. On the first day I had perfect lakeland weather and everything worked beautifully. I camped high in a stunning spot not far below the summit of Scafell Pike. The next day dawned wet and windy, which I had expected but the conditions deteriorated. The ViewRanger app didn't work, as I discovered I had not downloaded the maps. My compass played up, possibly because of the local geology. My custom-made map didn't give me enough surrounding detail for me to work out where I was. After several hours of being completely disorientated I bailed off the tops into a valley, where I flagged down the first car that passed. I found that I was three miles off my route and that it was 12 miles by road back to Helwith Bridge. Feeling completely deflated I gave up on my original plan and resigned myself to a long, wet walk of shame back to my car. Lady luck came to my rescue and the next car that passed me, moments later, offered me a lift all the way to Helwith Bridge. I learned a valuable lesson that weekend. Primarily to prepare better and not to be complacent.

Here on the Cape Wrath Trail I had my map and the ViewRanger app but I had not had a chance to test the app in anger. I was now well out of mobile reception range and was pleased to discover that it worked as it should. I had successfully downloaded the maps and a reassuring red cross on my phone screen marked my exact location on the OS 1:25k map. With a fresh flush of optimism I readjusted my chances of success back up to 50%.

I should take a moment to explain a couple of Scottish hill terms. Completely foreign to me until embarking on the Cape Wrath Trail, they became familiar parlance. A bealach is a mountain pass or col. The lowest point on a mountain ridge between two peaks. Allt appears to mean river in the Scottish Highlands.

I had originally thought of camping in Glen Cona before I crossed the bealach between Sgorr Craohh a Chaorainn and Meall nan Damh which led to Glenfinnan. Don't you just love Scottish hill names? There are so many more of them to come, and I find them really fascinating. Of course, being in Scotland, the place is littered with them!

The going was easy and the afternoon balmy. It felt lazy to stop at 3pm after only four and a half hours of walking, so I decided to keep going. At the point where the path started its ascent out of Glen Cona I passed Mark, another Cape Wrath Trail groupie, busily brewing up. I greeted him with a hearty, "Ow do?" and as he had his back to me and hadn't heard me coming, he half jumped out of his skin. I guess he thought he was safe in having the place to himself two hours' walk up a Scottish glen.

I hastily apologised for startling him and we introduced ourselves. Mark was in his early sixties and recently retired. He told me this walk was at the top of his bucket list. He'd been on the 8am ferry from Fort William and was taking it slowly. This wasn't his first stop for sustenance. He had decided it might be a shrewd idea to have his dinner before he tackled the pass. Looking at the map the bealach wasn't much higher than 300 metres. Before I headed off, he said he had checked the Cape Wrath bombing range website and the range was apparently active all of April and maybe May.

The Cape Wrath bombing range is the last hurdle before arriving at the lighthouse which marks the end of the Cape Wrath Trail. I hadn't even thought about calling the Ministry of Defence about their operations. It all seemed too far off and all that I had read suggested that it wasn't used at this time of year. I sort of noted the potential obstacle at the back of my mind. I still had well over 200 miles of Scottish Highlands to cross and it seemed a very long way away.

The climb over the bealach proved straightforward and it didn't seem too long before the terrain levelled out and began to descend. For whatever reason I have always managed the "ups" better than the "downs". Perhaps it was because of the warm day, but more likely because of my overladen pack, but on the way down I began to feel quite weary and my knees were beginning to whinge. I didn't want to stay in Glenfinnan and I felt I didn't have it in me to walk sufficiently beyond Glenfinnan to find a suitable wild spot to camp. All my attention turned to finding a place that was within a short walk of a water course and flat enough to make camp.

I found a place still high enough to enjoy fine views. Fortunately the winds aloft were sufficiently subdued for me to be able to appreciate my perch. I soon had the tent up, my bed made and my mac cheese supper bubbling on the stove. By some minor miracle I appeared to have packed everything I needed. In fact I found a few additional items that my youngest daughter had packed for me. The previous year on a similar walk my family had stashed mini chocolate eggs in any and every spare nook and cranny they could find. This year I found a couple of handmade mini cards with messages on them. One read "Happy Easter" and another "I love you". I found a third that read "Keep going!" This one I placed in my map case for encouragement.

Quaffing my wine (a significant but swiftly diminishing contribution to my heavy pack!) I thought of my family who were encouraging me each step of the way and marvelled at the scenery alight in the sunset. In a happy glow I allowed my chances of success to creep up to 70%.

I spent a few minutes reviewing my maps – the ground I had covered and what was coming up. I shuffled the used 28cm square map pages from my map case and loaded it with the next day's agenda. I scrawled a few notes on the back of the used maps. This was to become my new evening routine. By 9am I was tucked up in bed and fast asleep.

Looking back at Glen Cona.

First camp.

DAY 2

Just before Glenfinnan to Finiskaig overlooking Loch Nevis

Weather: Dry, increasing cloud cover throughout the day, light winds

22.1 miles, 1105 metres of ascent

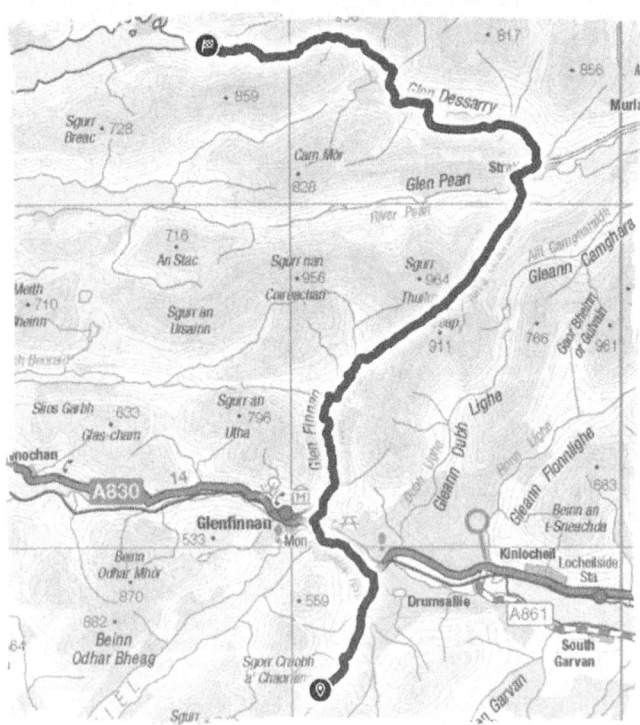

Another routine I was to embrace was a 2am ritual of re-inflating my mattress. I had invested in a Neo Air ¾ length sleeping air bed. When I had tested it, it had proven itself as lightweight and compact to carry, and also comfortable and warm to sleep on. Unfortunately, I suspect it was on one of my test weekends that it acquired a minor slow puncture. I remember camping late, up beyond Slippery Stones, north of Howden reservoir in the Peak District. I had parked at Langsett reservoir after work on a Friday evening. By the time I had crossed Cutt Gate, the dusk was gathering. With limited options I pitched my tent in a lovely riverside spot that I later found out was also a field of thistles. And, as the saying goes, the rest is history.

The mattress didn't completely deflate so it wasn't a real problem. As I was now of a certain age where I needed a nighttime pee, I was already awake enough to top up the mattress with a couple of puffs of air. On the subject of nocturnal wees, I realised I had forgotten one useful piece of kit which I had used extensively on previous walks but for whatever reason hadn't been on my kit list. I'm talking about a receptacle to pee into so I didn't have to leave the tent. Whilst I have read that others use a bottle, I have found that a heavy-duty bag that could stand up when full was much better as I could roll it up and pack it away more easily when not in use. Fortunately, I didn't experience nocturnal snow or rain, so nipping out of the tent to relieve myself wasn't too onerous. One small silver lining was that I got to see some stunning night skies.

I also experienced another novel problem on my first night. I was too hot. It was the first time in my limited history of wild camping that my sleeping bag was too warm for me. I know I sleep cold and usually don many layers and a down jacket to keep me warm at night. My strategy at home is to snuggle up to my wife who sleeps hot and feels like she has her own personal power station within her; she radiates heat. Shedding all my layers and unzipping the sleeping bag was new territory for me.

I was awake early and was surprised how swiftly I had adjusted to my new walking time zone. I enjoyed my Ready Brek with added sultanas for breakfast. I was packed up and on my way by 6am and was immediately aware that my knees, specifically my left knee, were not happy. General blisters, aching and discomfort can be managed. Knees, however, are more critical in the walking process. The previous day's induction coupled with an overweight pack had done them no favours. My knees had noted the extra weight. Whilst my brain had been preparing for this walk for the best part of a year, my body had been in blissful ignorance. My body had probably passed off the first day of the Cape Wrath Trail as a day hike that occasionally happened and it was no doubt expecting to be subsequently rewarded with a soak in a hot bath and a few days of rest. When day two of the Cape Wrath Trail arrived with more of the same physical regime but none of the reward, it slowly dawned on my body the part it had to play in this caper. Thus the twinging knee.

Knackered knees can easily result in a DNF (Did Not Finish). The situation was not good, as it was potentially fatal to completing the Cape Wrath Trail. I painfully remembered a two-day walk I'd done, walking the first part of the Pennine Way. I had been so full of vim and vigour that I had practically run up Jacob's Ladder and around to

Kinder Downfall crossing the Kinder plateau. That day, after stopping for lunch, my knees hurt like hell. I spent the next day and a half hobbling to the M62, heavily relying on my walking poles for support. It had then taken another week of rest for my knees to recover. I reduced my Cape Wrath Trail chances of success down to 20%.

This time my strategy was to ignore the problem as well as I could and crack on regardless. I gingerly limped the remaining couple of miles down to Glenfinnan and hoped beyond hope that by some miracle my knee wouldn't get any worse. Alas, when I passed the Glenfinnan Visitor Centre it was a good hour before its 10am opening time. As much as I thought they were missing a trick by not catering to the early-bird walker, the café remained stubbornly closed and devoid of life. During a short stint of road walking, a Land Rover tore past me and the driver, a tweed-clad gentleman precariously leaning out of the window, bellowed "Cape Wrath's that way!" with his thumb energetically pointing up the glen.

With that I turned off the road and made my way up Glenfinnan. I had a Cape Wrath Trail landmark to look forward to – the viaduct crossing the River Finnan, which is better known for its cameo in the Harry Potter films. Well, it's kind of impressive. But when you've walked the Yorkshire three peaks a few times and meandered below the Ribblehead viaduct, which in my humble opinion is much more spectacular, the Glenfinnan viaduct is a bit of an anti-climax. There wasn't even a sniff of the Hogwarts Express and there were no flying Ford Anglias. I made a mental note to write a letter of complaint to JK Rowling and Visit Scotland, the Scottish tourist board.

Not much further up Glenfinnan is Corryhully Bothy. This is almost as fabled on the Cape Wrath Trail as the aforementioned viaduct, because this bothy has electricity. The bothy is idyllically located next to the river. This is where I bumped into Mark again and learned that he'd passed my tent the previous evening. Mark may not be the fastest of walkers but it was clear that with his ability to start early and walk for many hours, he could cover the miles. I also met a single mum and her daughter who were staying in the bothy for a couple of days. For their Easter holiday they were driving close to, and then walking and staying in, bothies in the Highlands. A very creative and cost-effective holiday.

In case you are not familiar with the concept of bothies, let me fill you in. At their most basic level they are unlocked shelters in remote country, free of charge to use by those who love wild places. Many are maintained by the Mountain Bothy Association, which is run by volunteers. And occasionally there are places like Corryhully Bothy, a private estate bothy, where you can stay for a nominal fee. The bothy ethos is that all are welcome, and those that frequent these places are often of a kindred spirit.

At the Corryhully Bothy I also came across the speeding Land Rover that had passed me in Glenfinnan that morning but this time moving at a more sedate pace. The tweed-clad driver introduced himself as the estate manager and turned out to be quite a character. He had spoken to Mark earlier in the morning and Mark had told him that he was walking the Cape Wrath Trail. This explained the drive-by greeting he had hurled at me from the road. He outlined his part in maintaining and managing the local area. He even offered me a lift further up the glen, but then swiftly retracted the offer, noting that it would defeat the whole point of getting to Cape Wrath.

It was shaping up to be another beautiful day. The wind was light and the temperature was refreshingly cooler than the previous day. I bid farewell to the estate manager and Mark and moseyed up the glen. Heading towards the pass between Streap and Sgùrr Thuilm, I was aware that in the next few days I would be in remote terrain. Crossing the roadless rough bounds of Knoydart, I wondered how sensible this was with a potentially fragile knee. The pain had not become worse and if anything was subsiding. Either that or I was just getting used to it. I decided to employ the age-old strategy of hoping for the best.

At the top of the bealach the views to the north, across to Gleann a' Chaorainn, were breathtaking. I stopped to drink in the landscape and took a draught of water from near the source of Allt a' Chaorainn. I carefully picked my way down into the glen, making good use of my walking poles to minimise the impact on my knees. For the first time on the walk I was beginning to feel the remoteness of the land I was in. And I was loving it. What was potentially inhospitable territory because of its inaccessibility and reputation for grim weather was both beautiful and welcoming. Not for the first time I counted my blessings. The looming prospect of a potentially dangerous river crossing turned out to be a doddle. Allt a' Chaorainn was tame and I took pleasure in picking my way across stones that would normally be a foot under water. I found the game so much fun that I crisscrossed the river unnecessarily several times, just because I could.

Where I met the River Pean I was glad to find a bridge, as this was a significant watercourse. It was deep, wide and fast flowing. This is where I briefly said goodbye to the open views as I headed into a commercial forest along a well-made track. Forestry commission road walking can be dull, but after the previous couple of hours of trackless pathfinding down from the bealach and through the glen, I was happy for some easygoing plodding. Rounding a bend I passed a fellow walker taking a lunch break. I stopped to say hello. He introduced himself as Lucas and I learned that he was also on the Cape Wrath Trail but heading as far as Ullapool as he only had a week free. I left him to his sandwich and strolled on.

At around two in the afternoon I emerged from the forest and back into open country where I had expected to find another bothy, A' Chùil, nestled snuggly within Glen Dessarry. From my research, A' Chùil Bothy looked like a good place to spend the night if needed. As it turned out, the bothy wasn't next to the track but down a steep slippery path, and as by a small miracle my knees had all but stopped complaining, I decided to give it a miss. I did take advantage of the last of the trees for shelter to boil up some water for a Cup a Soup though. I was on my second soup when Lucas caught me up. He had had similar thoughts of staying at the bothy but, like me, had decided the day was too nice and the time was too early to stop now. He dropped his pack and detoured to recce A' Chùil.

By his return I had packed away my stove and was ready to go. He asked me if I'd like some company. I considered his offer. I enjoy walking by myself and hadn't come to the Highlands to meet people and make new friends. I swiftly decided, however, that if Lucas and I weren't compatible I could easily make my excuses and we could part company. I was also aware that the next section would be rough going. Iain Harper's guide said it was one of the toughest parts of the walk. The area had been used extensively for commando training in the Second World War. I reasoned a little company might not be a bad thing.

We had another bealach to cross before a steep descent to the shores of Loch Nevis, where yet another bothy was sited. The clouds had thickened and lowered. Some were draped on the hillsides each side of us, making it very atmospheric and a little moody. Happily the clag didn't get low enough to impede visibility and finally the temperature was sufficiently cool to be pleasant for hill walking.

Lucas and I chatted as we went. I learned that he was from Germany and had studied economics at St Andrews. He was currently mid PhD, exploring how macroeconomics and development could coexist in harmony with the natural world. A worthy field of study, I thought. His PhD was at the University of Leeds, but as he could work remotely he had opted to live in Glasgow to be closer to the Scottish hills. He was a keen hill walker and had climbed a few Munros, the term for Scottish hills above 3,000 feet. I was relieved to hear he wasn't a fanatical Munro bagger, as I liken these people to the trainspotters of the outdoor world who tended to be more interested in list ticking than actually enjoying the fresh air. Lucas had celebrated his 30th birthday a couple of days earlier with his wife and friends in Cona Glen. After celebrations, his wife and friends had headed back to Fort William whilst Lucas had continued along the Cape Wrath Trail.

I also discovered that he had spent the previous night at Corryhully Bothy with the single mum, her daughter, and Joe. Joe apparently was a voracious snorer.

The view down over Loch Nevis was welcome when it came, as it represented the end of the day's long walk. We still had the sharp descent to negotiate but confusingly the path led up. ViewRanger swiftly resolved my uncertainty. A little further along the indistinct higher path it became clear that if we had taken the obvious route down that followed the river, it would have quickly become precipitous. Over the centuries the flowing water had carved a deep impassable ravine that became increasingly severe with each metre it dropped towards the loch.

We contoured away from the river and then zig-zagged down into the glen. As the valley opened up the views were magnificent. The waters of the sea loch were a deep turquoise blue. On the shore stood Sourlies Bothy, a stone building with the dubious reputation of being the remotest bothy in the UK. A friend of mine who had stayed there had told me there was a large pan with the very specific purpose of cooking mussels that were freely available in the bay at low tide. Despite this culinary lure I decided to camp half a mile before the bothy. The tide was stubbornly in, making the prospect of mussel foraging slim. The bothy looked busy and I preferred to enjoy the scenery away from the crowds. Lucas was of the same mind, so we set up our small Highland outpost. Despite my misgivings, and to my surprise, I was enjoying his company.

I was about to fill up my water bladder from the obvious river that flowed down from where we had just come, when Lucas pointed out a rotting sheep carcass a few hundred metres up stream. I immediately diverted to a small tributary and thanked Lucas for his keen observation.

I mentioned my troublesome knees and expressed my amazement that they had settled down. Lucas told me his knees also occasionally complained, mainly after ascents taken too quickly. Knees are a perennial problem amongst hill walkers and therefore a regular topic of conversation. His experience was that his body took a day or two to adjust on a long walk, so maybe it was just my body adapting to the physical exercise. "Who knows?" I thought and quietly hoped my luck would hold. I reappraised my chances of completing the Cape Wrath Trail back up to 50%.

After dinner, bean feast bolognese and pasta for me and couscous for Lucas, we shared map time. Map time is the ritual amongst long distance walkers where you review the day's progress and look ahead to the challenges of the next morning. As we perused our maps, Joe came past. He mentioned that an engineer had condemned the Carnoch Bridge and insisted that it was removed because it was no longer safe. This left us with a potentially tricky river crossing early the next day.

Lucas asked if Joe would like to join us. I kept quiet as I knew canvas walls are no barrier to sound and Joe's snoring reputation was at the forefront of my mind. Fortunately he was set on sleeping at the bothy so we said our goodbyes and he wandered on.

Views to the north, across to Gleann a' Chaorainn.

Loch Nevis.

DAY 3

Finiskaig, Loch Nevis to just before Kinloch Hourn

Weather: Claggy and drizzling to start, becoming clear and fine by late afternoon

14.6 miles, 919 metres of ascent

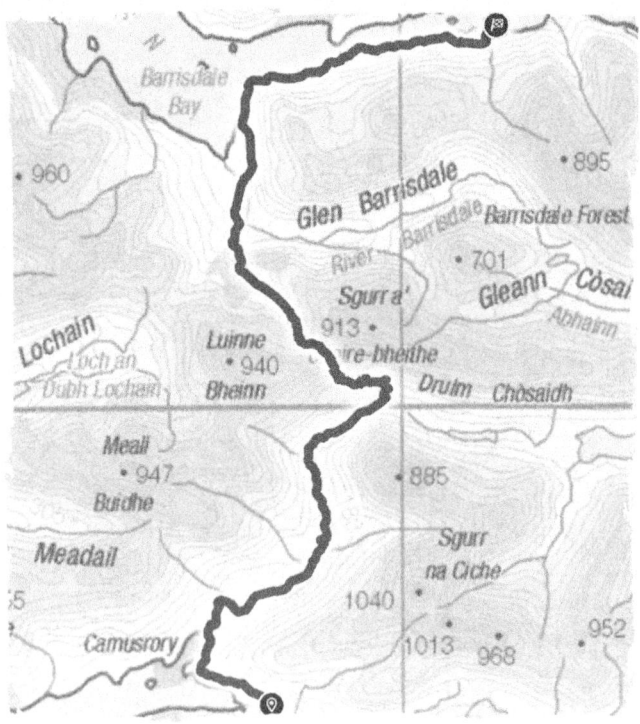

I woke around 5am and was breakfasted and packed by 6.30am just as Lucas was rising. We said our goodbyes and that we hoped to cross paths later down the track. It had rained a little during the night but the Scottish weather had the decency to pause its dampness whilst I struck camp. The drizzle soon resumed. Passing Sourlies Bothy I could hear the unmistakable rumble of Joe's snoring loudly resonating from the solid building. I had a brief chat with another of the bothy's inhabitants, who happened to be wide awake and making a morning coffee – a German chap who had flown to the UK the day before and then first bussed and then walked to the bothy. He had started the Cape Wrath Trail the previous year but bailed due to knee problems. "There but by the grace of God," my heathen brain thought. I wished him good luck and left him to be serenaded by Joe's snoring.

The next stretch offered easy walking along the beach when the tide was out. Alas, the tide was in, which left me the not-so-easy option of clambering up over the headland and then down into the next bay. With no real path and a precipitous drop to the rocks and sea below, my mind was soon focused. From my hard-fought early morning scramble I was rewarded with tremendous views. A lone stag heralded the sun as it crested the horizon. Priceless and almost worth the risk to life and limb.

In the next bay I ignored the guidebook which suggested I cross the boggy marshland to a bridge which I now knew was no longer there. Instead I kept to the edge of the quagmire, shadowing the hillside where the ground was a little less waterlogged. At a point where my less boggy detour became squelchy, I was able to skirt up onto higher ground to avoid soaking my boots. I didn't appear to have been the first person to have employed this tactic, as there was a semblance of a path. A mile or so up the bay the faint path headed to the River Carnoch where I could see a deer stalkers' track on the far side. Once again, because of the dry weather, it didn't take me long to find a way to cross and I didn't even need to take my boots off.

I paused to check my progress and the terrain ahead on the map. I unshouldered my backpack, as I kept my map rather inconveniently in its outside pocket. I also needed to retrieve my reading glasses that I now kept securely in the same pocket. Map checking was not as easy as I should have made it but it did at least ensure that I paused for a brief break every half an hour to an hour or so. Navigation appeared straightforward for the next few miles as all I had to do was follow the river.

I lazily bent down, grabbed my pack and started to swing it up onto my back. Halfway through this manoeuvre my spine started to twang with that most specific of pains that you only feel when you are about to pop a disc. I immediately let go of the backpack as if I had been jolted by an electric shock. Then, ever so slowly, I stood up straight. I'm not prone to back problems and thought it would be a huge irony if the first time I properly did my back in, I was at one of the most inaccessible places in all of the United Kingdom. After some mental probing I ascertained that the twinge of pain, unique to my vertebrae disintegrating, had subsided and I hoped I had done no permanent damage. This time, exercising extreme caution and following health and safety guidelines of bending my knees, I carefully hoisted my pack onto my back. It seemed that this time I had got away with it. I pondered that it probably wouldn't be the rivers, bogs and blisters that would defeat me on this walk but more likely the kind of thing that hits you out of the blue. I checked the sky carefully for falling grand pianos.

Following the meandering river the valley became narrower and its sides steeper until I was walking through a beautiful gorge. The trees were heavily clad in deep moss. The gorge felt ancient, and with mountains towering on all sides I could easily imagine it as the place that time forgot. It would have made a stunning spot to camp for the night, but as it was only mid-morning I settled for brewing up a tea and munching a Snickers.

I took the opportunity to check the map, as somewhere around there I needed to head north, ascending 300 metres vertically up a very steep, rough, trackless slope to hopefully intercept a clearly defined path. At least that is what the guidebook told me. It sounded easy enough, but with no landmarks and no path it could also be very easy to climb up out of the ravine in the wrong place and miss the well-defined path that was allegedly waiting for me. Discretion being the better part of valour, I fired up my phone, took a few photos of the stunning ravine and then checked where I was with ViewRanger. I was pretty much where I thought I was but it was so very reassuring to have it confirmed.

I started my climb upwards and noted that, surprisingly, paragliding, another passion of mine, had set me in good stead for exactly this scenario. Namely scrambling up steep trackless hillsides with a heavy bag on my back. I'd done this countless times over the last two decades when searching for a suitable launch. Only this time I wouldn't have the fun of flying off the top of the hill. And it was drizzling, which didn't happen when I went flying unless I had completely misjudged the weather. In these situations I have often used distraction to take my mind off my gasping lungs, my aching calves and the water running down my neck. I would employ mental arithmetic, doubling two, and keep doubling the answer to see how far I could get. I usually got up to around 16,384 before my brain began to hurt more than my calves and lungs. Or I would take myself off somewhere else within my mind. Anything that took me away from my immediate physical discomfort.

This has worked in the past, and it worked today, and it wasn't long before I reached the promised track and resumed my normal walking routine. The dampness thinned and my spirits lifted as I zig-zagged to the bealach at Mam Unndalain. Walking beyond the pass revealed Gleann Unndalain and Loch Hourn, another stunning sea loch and my second that day. It was a steady plod down to Barrisdale Bay. I monitored my back and knees closely for any sounds of grumbling. Thankfully they both kept schtum.

The skies had brightened but the wind was picking up, so I decided to delay lunch until I reached Barrisdale Bothy. Barrisdale Bothy is a well-appointed estate-owned bothy. It not only had electricity but also a flushing toilet. In these parts this represented the height of luxury. It comprised a couple of sleeping rooms with bunks and a kitchen come living room. There was a nominal fee of £5 to stay the night, but stopping for lunch was free.

Sheltering from the wind outside I made good use of the electric sockets to recharge my power bank. I "borrowed" some gas from a canister I found there to cook my noodles and brew up a hot chocolate. I also enjoyed eating my lunch at a proper table whilst seated on a real chair.

The guidebook intoned that whilst the route onwards from Barrisdale to Kinloch Hourn looked straightforward on the map, the reality was different on the ground, as it involved going along a fairly rough path with plenty of short, sharp climbs and descents. I contemplated this as I washed and stowed my stove. I was coming to the conclusion that, although I had been very fortunate with the weather, the guidebook liked to be a little melodramatic.

As I left the bothy Lucas arrived. We compared notes of the day's walking and both agreed that we had thoroughly enjoyed the wooded gorge and the mountain scenery as we'd climbed over the bealach. Lucas had already eaten his lunch somewhere up Gleann Unndalain and after a quick nosey around the bothy we walked on towards Kinloch Hourn. There were some ups and downs but the lochside path wasn't too rough and passed through more stunning scenery. It was the kind of terrain where I half expected a hobbit to jump out of the heather or to see a Viking long boat sailing up the loch.

I had set my sights on the hamlet of Kinloch Hourn that day but by 5pm my body was feeling the miles covered and more specifically the metres climbed. So when we rounded a headland, and a picture-perfect grassy beach appeared complete with a mountain stream offering fresh water, I promptly decided to stop and make camp for the night. I enjoyed another amiable evening sharing food and stories with Lucas. As the evening wore on, the clouds thinned and the sun burnished the hills in gold. The spectacular Highland setting was perfectly lit. We both agreed that we were incredibly lucky to be there to witness the Highland splendour.

Looking back at Loch Nevis in the morning mist.

Camping on the shores of Loch Beag.

DAY 4

Just before Kinloch Hourn to just beyond Morvich

Weather: Clear morning, turning into a sizzling afternoon but with significant winds high up

17.8 miles, 1302 metres of ascent

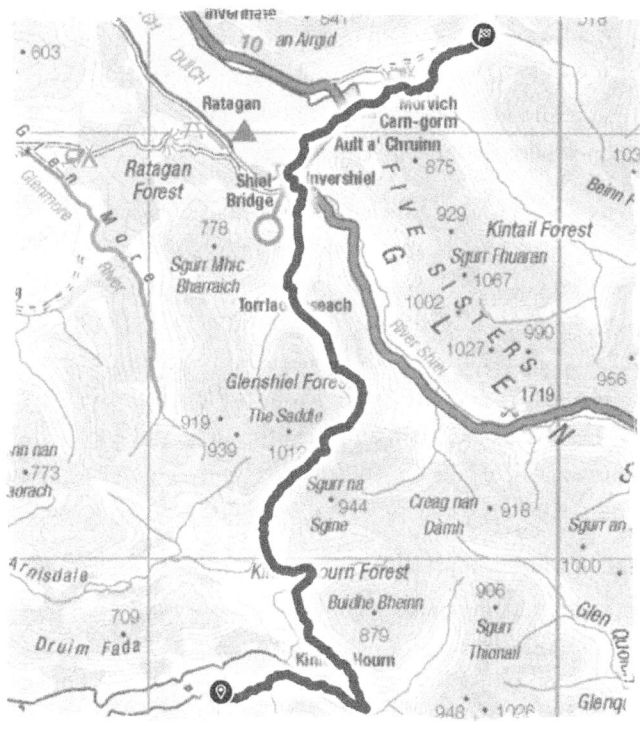

My walking routine was now well established and I was awake with the morning twilight and on my way by 6am. I said goodbye to Lucas and wished him luck. I didn't think we would meet again as he had a more relaxed schedule and was aiming to take in a summit or two on his last leg to Ullapool. He was heading back to Glasgow a couple of days earlier than he had originally planned in time to surprise his wife on her birthday.

It was another beautiful morning with a clear sky. The only cloud in sight was a flying saucer shaped lenticular hinting at high winds aloft. The dawn sun painted the heavens in purples, blues, pinks and oranges. The early morning stroll along Loch Beag was a joy. My physical niggles had not developed into serious issues. I was also becoming comfortable with seeing the mountains on the horizon and knowing that I would be going over and well beyond them by the end of the day.

Kinloch Hourn laid claim to less than a handful of houses but I'd read that one of them was a tea room and hoped to get a second breakfast there. Unfortunately, at 7am, the place was still asleep, so I ambled on. The route ascended up a hill through a wood and away from the loch along a reasonable 4x4 track. Towards the top of the first ridge I looked back across to the other side of the loch and could see where I'd camped. It looked quite a long way away. I was surprised at how swiftly the ground could be covered.

I stopped around 9am for a second breakfast of a second porridge and hot chocolate. My supplies were running low and there wasn't much to choose from. I was due to pick up my first resupply parcel at Shiel Bridge, which I hoped to reach by mid-afternoon. On the plus side my pack was about half the weight it had been when I'd set off, which made progress much swifter and easier on my body.

The guidebook suggested the next section might be challenging so I had a few M&M chasers. I looked into the bag of chocolate coated peanuts and experienced a moment of vertigo inducing dizziness. I had become so used to a natural colour palette of yellows, greens, greys and browns of the hills. The lurid primary colours of the M&Ms assaulted my senses. It took a moment to steady myself.

Suitably refreshed and with a mental note to eat the remaining M&Ms with my eyes firmly closed, I was off up the glen. The country was much more open and I could see how the magnificent mountainscape unfurled for miles. Hills all around stretching across the horizon. Despite the isolation and remoteness, I felt calm and unthreatened as I passed through the raw, rugged terrain. Maybe I had been a hunter-gatherer in these parts in a former life? Whatever it was, I was very much at peace in this visceral panorama.

Rounding the Munro, Sgùrr na Sgine, my next challenge came into view – Bealach Coire Mhàlagan, a pass at over 700m, the highest on the Cape Wrath Trail, with a very steep final approach. The guidebook claimed that the path would disappear and the next couple of miles would involve trackless route finding, hacking across boulder-strewn hillsides. I spotted a path that zig-zagged up the mountain before I needed to, but reasoned that it would be an easier climb on an existing path than no path further on and I could contour round from where this existing path ran out. It initially all went well and I gained height without too much effort; however, a mile or so later my chosen route became increasingly sketchy. I decided it would take too much time to retrace my steps so I pressed on. In the shadow of the impressive Forcan Ridge the terrain became much steeper and was pitted with near vertical slabs of rock the size of houses. Not a quaint bungalow-sized house either. More the size of a five-bedroom detached-size house. Significant detours were necessary. Add to the mix a fierce wind which seemed determined to peel me off the steep hillside and hurl me into the valley below, and finally sprinkle liberally with my fear of heights. I was now far from happy and way beyond my comfort zone. The fact that, if I slipped, nobody would find my smashed body for weeks, if ever, was the least of my problems.

With extreme focus I carefully placed each foot, fiercely concentrating on each considered step. I pushed the nausea to the back of my mind hoping my second breakfast wasn't about to decorate the hillside. "Just one more step, just one more step" became my mantra. It was probably less than an hour of shimmying around the hill before I crested the bealach with immense relief. Time plays tricks on you in these high-stress situations and it felt like I had been battling the mountain for days. I was shattered but elated. I took a few selfies to relieve the pressure and for me to show friends at a later date so I could claim, "That's me, and that's the ground I just covered. Isn't it amazing I didn't die?" Later, looking back at those photos, the hillside looks relatively benign… I didn't dare think what it would have been like to tackle that hurdle in adverse weather conditions.

I was happy that I had overcome the worst of the day's obstacles and it was, literally, all downhill from here, although it was still another six miles of downhill across more rugged and mostly trackless country to Shiel Bridge. From the bealach I followed the guidebook's instructions to the letter. Again, I was grateful for the near perfect weather. With minimal visibility, finding the route would have proved challenging. The minor problem I had to face was that it was a tad too warm. The fresh breeze helped cool me, but as I descended into the sheltered glen the heat rose.

I was following Allt a' Choire Chaoil, a sparkling mountain river. Maybe it was the heat? Maybe I was euphoric from surviving the last climb? Maybe it was the picture-perfect seductive pool of clear mountain water complete with its own idyllic waterfall? I'm not quite sure what possessed me, but for the first, and possibly the last, time in my life, I dumped my pack, stripped naked and plunged into the river. What seemed initially like a great idea immediately struck me as over-optimistic. Scottish mountain waters are baltic. I'd never gone from boiling to freezing so quickly. I probably lasted no more than three minutes before fleeing the water's icy clutches. I quickly dressed whilst checking no other walkers were unfortunate enough to witness my escapades. Skinny-dipping in the Highlands is overrated, even if it did offer the perfect opportunity to re-enact the 1980's Timotei shampoo ad.

Suitably refreshed and thawing from brain freeze I trundled the last few miles down to Shiel Bridge. I was mighty glad when the glen came into view and I passed the first people I'd seen since saying goodbye to Lucas. That morning seemed a long time ago.

The proprietor of Shiel Bridge service station and campsite turned out to be the least positive soul on this planet. In fact, perhaps I could be so bold as to suggest he might seek an alternative vocation rather than being the front man for tourists in that neck of the woods. Unless, of course, he was there to keep that particular neck of the woods free of tourists? In which case he could be a roaring success.

He had received my resupply parcel which he joylessly passed on to me. I also took the opportunity to liberate him of some of his limited but welcome additional supplies. Cheese, bread, bacon, eggs, steak pasty, orange juice, wine, brandy and chocolate. I paid the princely sum of £2.50 to use the campsite showers. Exiting the shop I devoured the steak pie, two improvised cheese rolls and a litre of orange juice. I also decanted the wine and brandy into the lightweight plastic bottles I had and discarded the glass bottles and any other superfluous packaging.

Discovering I had mobile reception, I fired off a few text messages to friends and family. It was the first time I'd been able to communicate via mobile phone since leaving Fort William, four days earlier. For safety reasons I had been carrying my friend's satellite tracker. On departure I had agreed to send a set message at the end of each day: "All good. I am camping here for the night." I had sent the message at the end of day one, forgotten to send it on day two and remembered to send it on day three. Luckily no one panicked and mobilised mountain rescue on day two. Phew. The satellite tracker also, not surprisingly, tracked my progress. This was dependent on me remembering to turn it on and the device having sufficient battery charge. After the second day I got into a routine of turning it on in the morning and activating the tracking, then sending the safety message, and turning it off in the evening. I found that the battery could probably last six days with this routine.

My wife immediately called back and it was great to catch up with her and my daughters. Yes, they had had a good Easter and all was well. No, they hadn't fretted when I'd forgotten to send the agreed set message on day two. This was mainly as they could see I was still making progress on the trackers' web page. I joked that I could have been eaten by a wolf, tracker and all, and that it was the wolf's movements that they had been following. My wife found this absurd. Not because there are no giant people-eating wolves in these parts, but for the fact that a wolf would not be following the Cape Wrath Trail. Completely logical of course. After a long chat I said goodbye and headed to the campsite facilities for a shower and a shave.

Having washed, eaten, restocked supplies and caught up with my family, I didn't feel the need to stay at a campsite. And after the brief dalliance with civilisation I felt ready to return to the wilds of Scotland. The decision to press on was easy. From Shiel Bridge to Morvich there was a short spell of road walking. Passing an open post office I took the opportunity to send a few postcards, hastily penned, balanced on top of an ice cream freezer. The afternoon was still hot and I gleefully guzzled several bottles of sweet, sugary carbonated drink I wouldn't normally dream of letting past my hallowed lips. They tasted great.

Passing the sporadic house and another campsite that constituted Morvich, the day was wearing on. As soon as it was decently possible to consider wild camping beyond

Morvich, I was scoping every potential opportunity. Unfortunately, where on the map there looked to be an abundance of ideal places beside a river, on the ground there was a high sturdy fence between these likely places and the footpath I was on. The map suggested that, if I didn't find a place to camp soon, I would be heading up through a commercial forest and over a bealach, which meant suitable camping opportunities would diminish further. Where the path dipped into the shallow canyon that the river flowed through, and just after crossing a footbridge, I found a place not much bigger than the very modest footprint of my tent. It was barely ten metres from the footpath but I reasoned that at 6pm there would be little traffic. It was a beautiful location and the ravine afforded shelter from the wind.

I enjoyed a feast of bacon, eggs, (rehydrated) onions and mash, all washed down with a plastic camping mug of fine Merlot. I even allowed my feet a soothing, if refreshing, soak in the river. It had been a tough day, both mentally and physically. Serenaded by the River Croe it wasn't long before I was fast asleep.

The Forcan Ridge approaching Bealach Coire Mhàlagan.

Looking down from Bealach Coire Mhàlagan towards
Shiel Bridge.

DAY 5

Just beyond Morvich to Strathcarron

Weather: Mainly cloudy, initially light wind but strengthening throughout the day

24.4 miles, 1556 metres of ascent

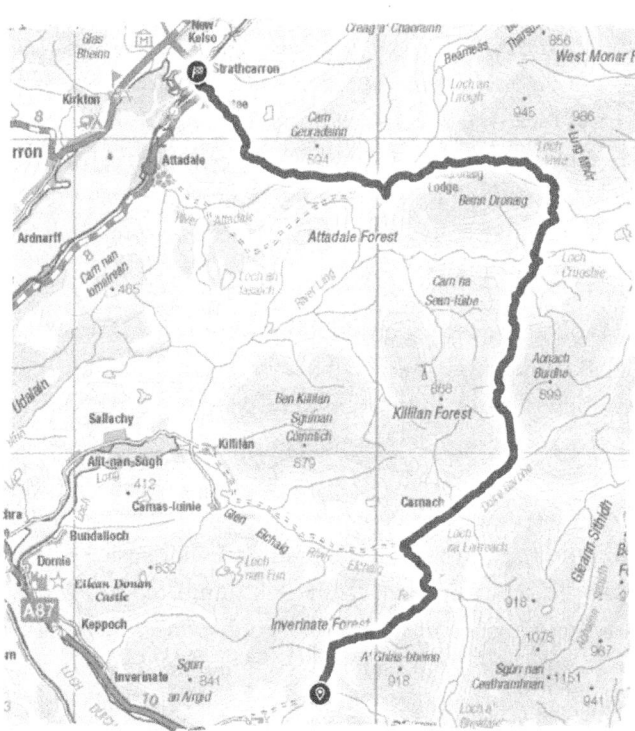

My standard porridge breakfast was supplemented by a couple of soft-boiled egg rolls liberally applied with seasoning that I'd thoughtfully included in the resupply parcel for just such an occasion. After four days of backpacking food, eggs and bread were a delicacy. I struck camp and tied the remaining two eggs to the back of my pack.

I was a little preoccupied with the next Cape Wrath Trail obstacle, namely the Falls of Glomach, or rather more accurately the path descending into the ravine that the Falls of Glomach had carved out over the millennia. According to Wikipedia, this waterfall, with a drop of 113 metres, is ranked the third highest in the UK. I had read on various blogs that the route down is precipitous to say the least. In my mind's eye I envisaged a six-inch ledge etched out of a vertical rock face that I would need to traverse and where one slip meant certain doom. I am not fond of heights and I am less fond of plummeting to my death. But I wasn't there yet, so I employed my usual ostrich tactic of completely ignoring the problem, and I put it out of my mind.

I found the early morning hike up through Dorusduain Wood therapeutic. I usually hold tramping through commercial forest in the highest disdain, but that morning, given what lay ahead, the mundanity was soothing. Even the crossing of Bealach na Sròine felt like a stroll in the park. I began to feel the tension in me grow as I descended from the pass. The scenery felt raw and once again remote. I passed a tent whose occupants still slumbered in a beautiful, if exposed, spot. A sign confirming my arrival at the top of the Falls of Glomach compounded my fear, with its message "DANGER. Please take great care," in letters larger than the falls' name. I declined to take the short path down to the viewing platform as I was so focused on overcoming what lay before me.

Where the water plummeted into oblivion I bumped into another Cape Wrath Trail walker – a Scottish woman, Rowena, who had walked the trail a few years earlier. On her first trip she had been accompanied by her (now ex) partner who had no head for heights and so they had taken a long circuitous detour. A detour I wanted to avoid but was also prepared to accept if the way down was as bad as the hype. I explained my reservations and she offered to metaphorically hold my hand. I declined, claiming that I didn't want any witnesses when I was balling my eyes out in terror, clinging to the hillside halfway down. But as we were both going the same way at the same time we descended together. As it turned out, the hype was mostly hype. Yes, the path was steep. Yes, a misplaced foot could have probably been your last. But no, it wasn't only fit for the reckless mountain goats. The path was clear enough and I have traversed far worse. Having a fellow walker to chat to on the way down helped me not to dwell on the "what ifs", and before I knew it the incline became shallower and we were approaching Loch na Leitreach.

Nearing the River Elchaig, and with a huge mental hurdle behind me, I said goodbye to Rowena. I told her I was stopping for a brew and wished her well with her journey. It had now been several hours since breakfast and I was ready for a break. I also wanted some space and time alone. I appreciate that there are benefits of walking with others; however, it is a different kettle of fish to strolling by myself amongst my own meandering thoughts. And at that moment I was happy to have some solitude. The river was mesmerising, the tea heartening, the Snickers nourishing and the relief was, well, relieving.

I felt as if a weight had been lifted from me. I was over another of the Cape Wrath Trail hurdles. Perhaps I could finish this walk? With a bounce in my step and a new-found feeling of invincibility I headed on. The going along a 4x4 track was easy and the wayfinding was straightforward, along the glen and over a relatively shallow bealach between two Highland ridges. I decided to listen to some music. I had refrained before now as I didn't want to consume valuable battery juice and listening to tunes seemed a tad frivolous. I had been walking with my phone turned off and I only powered it up when I wanted to take a photo or check my navigation on ViewRanger, and even then the phone was on airplane mode. After four and a half days it still had 50% battery. My other electronic device, the Garmin InReach tracker, also registered 50% battery despite being on continuously whilst I walked. I carried a powerbank and at 350 grammes it was not an inconsiderable addition to my kit. I had not yet used the powerbank so it was still fully charged and good for four plus recharges of my phone or tracker. I decided that perhaps I was being too cautious with my juice and felt a little frivolity wasn't going to jeopardise my chances of success.

Having had no stimulus for days apart from physical exertion and the nature around me, the power of music hit me like a lightning bolt. The Spotify playlist that I had listened to hundreds of times over the past few years sounded incredibly fresh and blindingly vibrant, as if I was hearing the music for the first time. The tunes filled me and lifted my spirits. I hit my stride. I found my zone. That early afternoon I felt like I was flying. As if I was standing still and the landscape was passing me. Like the special effects in the early black and white films where the actors were sitting in a stationary car pretending to be driving and the backdrop was wound round on a large horizontal roller behind them.

Crossing the bealach and heading down to Loch Cruoshie I felt tears running down my cheeks. I was crying uncontrollably. My first instinct was to stifle the tears and check to see if anyone could see me crying. I had conditioned myself throughout my life to hide emotion. To be a man, whatever that meant. Emotion signified weakness. I intuitively sensed that social conditioning didn't matter where I was at that point in my life, both mentally and physically. I briefly inwardly examined the source of this emotion and almost immediately realised the tears were tears of joy. The sheer pleasure and wonder of where I was. Exactly in that moment. I am not a man of faith but I recognise spirituality when it hits me. A colossal slap across my face. My heathen soul found religion. Mother nature was my God. The Scottish Highlands were my church. And "Good Feeling" by Flo Rida was the hymn of the moment.

In this euphoric state the miles flew by and I soon found myself approaching the perfectly situated Maol Bhuidhe Bothy on the shores of Loch Cruoshie. In my planning I had vaguely thought of stopping there for the night. It was a beautifully kept building in its own private remote glen. The bothy logbook recorded that a maintenance party had recently been and installed a skylight in the main living area which transformed it from a dingy room to a bright and airy place. At 1pm it was far too early to call it a day and I was feeling surprisingly fresh and invigorated considering the previous day's mileage and ascents. I settled for a lunch break of noodles and Cup a Soup.

At the bothy I caught up with Rowena, who had also been taken by the beauty and wonder of the surroundings we were in and it was a pleasure to share our mutual joy. I also met Alex, a chap in his early twenties, who had caught the £40 sleeper train up from London. He was using the bothy as a base to bag the surrounding summits over the Easter break. Alex was a professional ballet dancer and he considered moving through the wilds of Scotland to be not too dissimilar to dancing. The flow of movement, the balance and poise of each step. I may not possess any ballet skills but I completely understood what he was saying.

Alex had walked on the previous day from the direction I was heading. He suggested an alternative route which took advantage of recently built unpaved roads and avoided some of the trackless bog hopping. The roads had been made to aid hydro work going on in the area. I took his advice and headed off, leaving Alex and Rowena sitting on the bench outside the bothy soaking up the views. My first task was to cross the river that flowed into the loch. Despite the dry weather it was still a substantial watercourse and I considered that for the first time I might need to employ my river crossing strategy, namely putting on my as yet unused trail shoes that I had been carrying. In the end I was able to carefully hurl a few well-chosen rocks into the river to create impromptu stepping stones. My trail shoes remained dry and packed in my backpack. I enjoyed an hour of trackless route finding as I circumferenced Beinn Dronaig and crossed another river before connecting with the hydro tracks. It was fairly breezy but the wind was pleasantly warm.

Checking the ViewRanger app I became very disorientated as I was nowhere near the red line of the track I had preloaded before I'd set off. The same red line I had been following for days and which had become very reassuring. I was several miles off route and it took me a moment to realise why. The alternative route Alex had suggested had taken me anticlockwise around Beinn Dronaig, the opposite way to the suggested track. After checking my map I soon worked out what was going on, where I was and where I was headed.

I passed a Dutch family who were also walking the Cape Wrath Trail. A mum and her two teenage kids had walked the West Highland Way several years earlier and found it too touristy. They had returned to Scotland the previous year to walk the Cape Wrath Trail but had been thwarted by very wet weather and had had to give up at Shiel Bridge. This year they had come back to finish it. I wished them luck and pressed on. I reached Bendronaig Lodge, a fine estate bothy, around four in the afternoon. It was an ideal place to stop for the night but I felt compelled to keep going. It was a further eight miles to Strathcarron and although I could wild camp before then, the exposed high ground and the strong wind made that option unlikely. My lightweight tent was amazing but I didn't rate its chances pitted against 50mph gusts of wind. There was also the lure of real food and a proper bed for the night, as I knew there was a hotel in Strathcarron.

My walking zeal from earlier in the day had all but faded as I hacked my way over Bealach Alltan Ruairidh. I was happy that my body hadn't crumpled under the punishing pace I'd set it, but my legs were weary and I was beginning to stumble more often than I should. The Highland moonscape dotted with lochans continued to shine, although in my fatigued state I was growing numb to it. The last few miles of the day were a long slog and seemed to take forever. I had to push myself with all my mental strength.

I was hugely relieved and completely knackered when I entered the hotel and lumbered up to the bar that evening. I asked about the possibility of a room, but at £90 I decided my money would be better invested in food and wine, and opted to pay £15 to camp. Richard, the owner, had turned his back on the corporate world and bought the Strathcarron Hotel six months earlier. It had become run down by the previous owner and he was in the process of refurbishing and rebuilding its reputation. Richard was an affable host and supplied me with a fresh towel as he showed me the shower room and took my dinner order. The restorative powers of a burger and wine gave me just enough strength to put up my tent, make my bed and crawl into my sleeping bag. After 12 hours on my feet and 25 miles under them I was soon fast sleep and oblivious to the tent cloth flapping in the wind.

At the top of the Falls of Glamoch.

Red deer

Maol Bhuidhe bothy on the shores of Loch Cruoshie.

DAY 6

Strathcarron to below Sail Mhòr

Weather: Overcast and windy

16.3 miles, 1264 metres of ascent

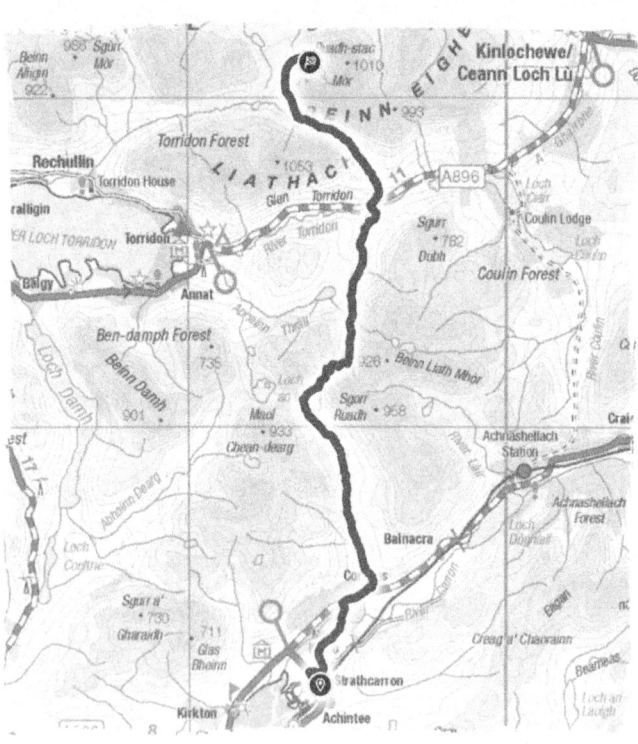

My day started at its usual early hour, which was unfortunately a little too early for the 7am breakfast I had ordered the night before. After showering, packing, brewing up and drinking hot chocolate, checking my maps and then checking them again it was still only 6.30am. I was the only person in the breakfast dining room when I arrived and availed myself of the muesli and yogurt whilst waiting for my Scottish breakfast.

During this walk I had actively encouraged myself to eat as much as possible. I discovered that I had underestimated what I would need to eat in a day. Fortunately, because my pace was much swifter than I had planned and I was covering ground much quicker, I had spare food. I was essentially eating the food I had planned for six days walking in four days, but this didn't matter as I was also covering the miles I planned for six days in four days so it was all working out. I also took full advantage of topping up supplies at the shops and eating at the pubs I passed. In six days of walking, these facilities came to the grand total of one shop in Shiel Bridge and one pub, the Strathcarron Hotel.

The Scottish breakfast was the fry-up you would imagine. As well as haggis, it included something new to me, in the form of two hefty square sausages, or Lorne sausage to give it its proper name. It was fair to say I was stuffed to the gills by the time I polished my plate with the last of my toast. My legs were also aching from the miles that had been walked, so it was with a peculiar shuffling waddling gait that I set off from the hotel, only to return half an hour later to retrieve the fresh milk Richard had kindly given me and that I had accidentally left on my breakfast table. I'm not sure whether it was my love of a proper cup of tea with fresh milk or that an extra mile when I was walking 240 of them seemed insignificant, but I didn't begrudge the additional distance to retrieve the milk.

Conveniently, the first few miles of the day along the River Carron were gentle, as I felt decidedly queasy from breakfast. After an hour my stomach settled down and my legs limbered up. I left the sparsely scattered houses that represented civilisation behind me and veered off up another picturesque Scottish glen flanked by more majestic peaks. Another well-kept bothy, Coire Fionnaraich, appeared in time for elevenses.

Bealach Ban beckoned. I plugged myself into the chilled hypnotic tribal beats of Badmash and Shri. Breathing in the stunning raw Highland landscape, I lost myself in time floating up the wild glen. I felt happy to be alive, and humble and privileged to be there. I was immensely grateful for having the good fortune and chance to be where I was. Cresting the pass, even more stunning Scottish landscape was revealed. Glen Torridon had an ancient feel to it and its scale is huge. The moment felt endless, but it eventually waned as my legs, feet and knees reminded me of the miles I was covering. Once again I was beginning to stumble more than I should and I spent extra time carefully placing my feet.

I stopped for a late lunch next to the Ling Hut near the road that ran along the valley floor. Chewing a peperami sausage I considered my options for the day. There was a fierce easterly wind, and where I was sitting was too exposed to camp. Despite my tired body it also felt too early to stop. Pressing on to Kinlochewe would make it a very long day and the last six miles would be into a ferocious headwind. I would arrive there too late and exhausted to make the most of the facilities and shops that this Highland oasis offered. It felt counterintuitive to keep going and camp short, halfway from where I was to Kinlochewe. It would leave me camping high up, which would potentially amplify the already strong winds. Looking at the map I reasoned that I could hopefully camp in the lee of a substantial lump of rock, Sail Mhòr, another Munro. My default position was to keep going when in doubt.

Crossing the A896 and passing a car park, I saw a deer. I had seen plenty of deer on this trip but all of them had been very shy and scampered away as soon as I got within a sniffing distance of them. This particular deer was being hand fed bread and allowing people to take selfies with her. It was a tad surreal and I wondered how this deer had become so tame. There was something else different about this deer. I'm no expert, but it looked more like a reindeer than the red deer I had passed. I took a quick photo to confirm what I was seeing and that I wasn't hallucinating, and then I headed up Coire Dubh Mòr.

Walking up the glen towards Sail Mhòr, the valley acted like a wind tunnel, making it tough going. I passed a few walkers with their heads down braced against the wind. All of them were heading out of the hills and on their way home. All of them gave me questioning looks, wondering why I was going the other way. As it turned out, when I arrived at Loch Coire Mhic Fhearchair, there were no less than four tents already pitched. It was a beautiful setting, with the loch couched below three Munros and a multi-tiered waterfall running from the loch into the valley. At

600 metres height the expansive views to the west were breathtaking. Walking up the waterfalls towards the loch I met a couple coming the other way. Andy, a Scottish chap, and his partner Virginie, who was French. They were also walking the Cape Wrath Trail and told me not to bother heading further up as any suitable pitches had already been taken. I didn't mind, as there was plenty of room lower down, although it was a little more exposed.

With the tent pitched, I found a mildly sheltered place to cook up my dinner. Mac cheese and chorizo was still my favourite despite overdoing it on previous walks. On Andy's suggestion I headed up to the top of the falls for sunset to take in the panorama across Wester Ross. Of all the wild camp locations this was by far the most amazing. The mountain vista stretched far to the horizon and the twilight cast a magical hew to the landscape. The price of this beauty was a sleepless night, as the wind raged and battered my tent. Every few minutes a particularly aggressive gust would flatten the tent to the ground before it bounced up once more. I began to think of my tent as a Weeble, as in the "Weebles wobble but they don't fall down" children's toy from the eighties. I didn't rate the tent's chances of surviving the night and had visions of packing away a tattered mess in the morning.

Glen Torridon.

Wester Ross. My tent is in the lower centre.

DAY 7

Below Sail Mhòr to Kinlochewe

Weather: Damp, claggy start to the day, then brightening up

7 miles, 205 metres of ascent

Not surprisingly, I was awake, up and packed early. To my amazement the tent sustained no damage. I had a new-found admiration for this lightweight marvel of a mobile home. The day started grey. Low cloud shrouded the previous day's magnificent views. The clag gave an ominous feel to the hills.

It was tough going across trackless rock-strewn ankle-snapping terrain and I was glad I hadn't tried to cover it the previous day. Even after a night's semi-rest, both navigation and walking were a challenge. Once again I relied heavily on ViewRanger to find my way. I felt a bit of a fraud for not using solely my map and compass for navigation, but the reassurance ViewRanger gave me was a godsend. It also meant less stopping to check the map and that I could focus more of my attention on where I was placing my feet. After a three and a half hour slog I descended out of the hills to the metropolis of Kinlochewe.

Kinlochewe boasted a campsite, post office, petrol station and hotel. More importantly, it was home of the hotel that I had sent my second supply parcel to. They had only accepted my package on the condition that I booked a room or a bed in the bunkhouse. I had explained that my itinerary could not be guaranteed due to the nature of walking such distances and the vagrancy of the weather. They had suggested I book a bed in the bunkhouse as they could be flexible on when I arrived. This was fortunate, as I arrived two days ahead of schedule. After enquiring about the possibility of upgrading from bunkhouse to hotel room, the £110 price tag put pay to my ambitions. I explained that I'd prefer not to sleep in the bunkhouse and asked if it was possible to camp instead? I had a perfectly good tent and I preferred the tranquility and peace of my own space to the point where I was prepared to forget the £20 and head off back into the Scottish wilds. The chap at the hotel was most understanding and agreed that he too would prefer to camp rather than share a room with a bunch of snoring strangers. He agreed that I could camp in the hotel gardens for £10 and use the £10 surplus credit towards an evening meal. Sorted. The restaurant opened at 6.30pm and I said I'd see him then.

With digs taken care of, I took stock of provisions and equipment. My first sortie to the post office and shop procured bacon, eggs, mushrooms and croissants for lunch, and a few postcards to scribble. Suitably sated I then turned my attention to my much neglected personal hygiene. I had had two showers in the past four days so wasn't doing too badly but I also hadn't washed my clothes for seven days. The clothes I had been walking and sweating in. And the combination of sultry days and tough ascents meant there had been a significant amount of sweat. Thanks to the wondrous properties of Merino wool I wasn't truly minging, or maybe I'd just become inured to my personal whiff? Anyway, I decided I should do some overdue laundry. This consisted of trampling my clothes in the shower tray whilst I washed myself. I may even have rubbed a bit of soap on them but suffice to say the laundry process was rudimentary. As I had decided that only the essentials needed attention, I washed a grand total of one pair of socks, one pair of boxer shorts and my base layer. Once done, I pitched my tent and bedecked the guy lines with my laundry like Buddhist prayer flags flapping in the breeze, well, maybe only in my mind.

Fed and with ablutions taken care of, and my shelter for the night sorted, I opened my supply package to reacquaint myself with what I'd packed two weeks earlier. I quickly shed what I didn't need, which wasn't much (a portion of dehydrated onions and a mini pack of wet wipes), then headed back out to the post office come shop for what I was lacking. That's right, red wine and brandy. Plus the marginally less essential camping gas canisters.

Back at the bunkhouse communal kitchen I sat down to gather my thoughts. Spreading out my 28cm square map pages across the large table, piecing them together like a jigsaw to create a narrow corridor north across Scotland, I became aware that I was halfway. When I had initially considered walking over 240 miles across the beautiful badlands of Scotland, I wasn't able to dare think that I could actually make it. It was just too far, the challenge too great, the magnitude for disaster too overwhelming. But there, at the bunkhouse kitchen table I began to let myself believe it was possible. I didn't like to dwell too long on the possibility of success as that would surely jinx it.

My thoughts then turned to the hurdle of the Cape Wrath bombing range and I recalled the conversation I had had with Mark all that time ago, on the first day in Cona Glen. I dug out the Ministry of Defence (MOD) number and dialled. To my surprise a clipped, well-spoken, proficient voice answered. A no-nonsense kind of voice that you could trust. I explained I was walking the Cape Wrath Trail and that I was halfway. "Can I cross the bombing range next Friday?" I blurted. I thought he was incredibly understanding and wondered how many random phone calls from excitable walkers he had to handle each day.

He explained that the range was technically "active" on Friday, but with the way things had been going, there was a good chance that operations would have ceased by then. I thanked him profusely and remained in awe that the armed forces had time for vagabond walkers whilst orchestrating airborne havoc that wreaked significant destruction.

Taking full advantage of the mobile phone reception, I checked in with my family, who were having fun at the opposite end of the UK in West Somerset, hanging out with my wife's mum and dad. I also checked in with my support and retrieve team, aka my brother-in-law David. The original plan was to meet him as I passed through Kinlochbervie and that we would both hike to Sandwood Bay. From there I would head to Cape Wrath to finish the walk and he would backtrack to Kinlochbervie where he would pick up his car and drive round to pick me up at Durness. The tincy wincy logistical issue was that at the rate I was walking, I might well make goal before he had set off from home. The message I received from David was "Slow down and enjoy the views!" Easier said than done when you have a problem with sitting still.

On checking Facebook I discovered my friend Neil, whose tracker I was using, had been posting daily screen grabs charting my progress. There were many kind messages of support and I was reminded of all the friends and family that were behind me. As remote and as long as this walk was, they were with me every step of the way. The posts had also increased my fundraising tally. Thank you Neil!

Feeling about as organised and prepared as I could be, I started to catch up on making a few notes. Beyond eating and a bit of map time each evening, my routine included scrawling notes on the day's misadventures. With the uncharacteristic long days I had been doing, my note-taking had suffered. I had been recycling my square tiles of maps as notepaper. On a good day I would cover the back of two squares with compact script. On the more recent longer days I had barely covered half a side, just with a few bullet points that I hoped would aid my memory at a later date. I'm not entirely sure why I keep a diary when on a long distance walk. I don't keep a diary in everyday life. Maybe I aspire to be some kind of outdoorsy journalist? I have shared my rambling thoughts of previous walks, and to my knowledge I can claim to have only two interested parties. My father-in-law and a friend, fellow walker and linguist, Dawn. I kid myself that perhaps my children might be interested in what I do and what it is like to hack across a wilderness for many days self-supported. But I suspect the real reason for my ramblings is much more mundane. Writing about my trials and tribulations is my therapy.

My writing and reverie was interrupted by the arrival of Andy and Virginie. We were of kindred spirit and it felt like meeting old friends, even though we had first met just the previous evening. We compared experiences of the morning's boulder-strewn traipse and concluded that it hadn't been very pleasant. They gently made fun of me when I transferred the wine and brandy I had bought from glass bottles to the plastic bottles I carried to save weight. Surely carrying so much wine and brandy defeated the ethos of backpacking light? Then they admitted that being professional photographers they each carried three cameras plus batteries and various photographic paraphernalia. Each to their own, I thought.

They also mentioned that the hotel's restaurant was going to be busy and that they had booked for 6.30pm. I was struck by panic and wondered if my "See you when the restaurant opened" had been taken as a booking. I hot tailed it to the hotel reception, where a lady checked the restaurant booking sheet. No reservation could be found. The next available offer was 8pm, not far off my new accustomed bedtime. With a sigh, I agreed.

I arrived at the restaurant at the somewhat optimistic time of 7.15pm and was met by the chap who I had seen when I had first arrived that morning at the hotel. He gave me a withering look and informed me that I had missed my 6.30pm slot and that they were extremely busy. I was now at the back of the queue. I tried to explain my conversation with the lady earlier and suggested that perhaps there had been a misunderstanding. He was stressed and uninterested. On trying to order I was told that they were out of burgers and chips so I went for whatever they could give me. Given my options I resigned myself to a long wait and ordered a glass of wine. Miles, another Cape Wrath Trailer who I had spoken to earlier, had had the foresight to correctly book a table and was just finishing his soup entrée. He beckoned me over to join him. Moments later his main course of burger and chips arrived. I was salivating. Miles exclaimed that he had ordered fish and chips and did not want what had been brought out from the kitchen. I heroically stepped into the breach and claimed the misplaced ordered dish. I had snaffled my prize and bid Miles good night just as his fish and chips finally arrived and I silently thanked my guardian angel.

On my way to bed I passed a couple enjoying a

celebratory night cap at a patio table in the hotel garden. They had just completed the first half of the Cape Wrath Trail and were heading home the next day. They invited me to join them for a brandy. They hailed from London, but the girl was a born and bred Yorkshire lass now working in the charity sector. The bloke was original East End blood and on a mission to introduce more trees and develop green spaces in our capital city. Both interesting and inspirational people. They also imparted their ideas for making backpacking cuisine gourmet. They recommended a flavourful, potent caper, anchovy and garlic sauce to mix in with pasta and a powerful powdered coconut, dried chilli, ginger, onion and shrimp paste masala to cook up with noodles for a va va voom laksa. After eating fairly staid stodge on my backpacking trips, this was truly food for thought.

Scottish lichen.

DAY 8

Kinlochewe to Shenavall

Weather: Dry and cloudy with a moderate breeze

18.5 miles, 1074 metres of ascent

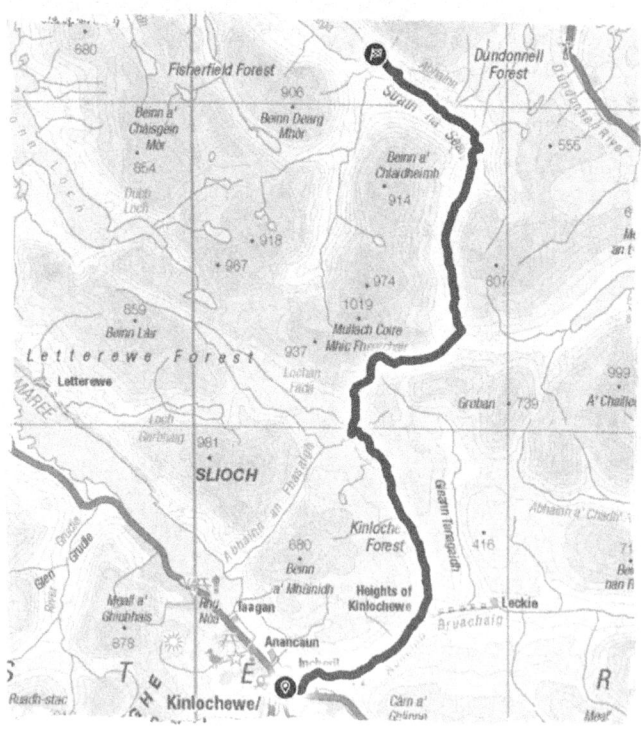

Despite the relatively late night I was up and at 'em early.
I met Andy and Virginie in the kitchen with their stuff
spread out from corner to corner. Being professional
photographers I guess they were underpinning their
creativeness. I claimed a small space in a corner of the
kitchen that their stuff hadn't quite reached and snaffled
my customary porridge, supplementing it with a delicious
bacon butty. I was surprised to hear that they set an alarm
to facilitate their early starts as my internal body clock
seemed sufficient to arrest my slumber. They confessed that
they would have preferred camping to the bunkhouse, as
various nocturnal movements, creaking beds and slamming
doors had made it far from a restful environment. I
commiserated with them both, then bid them a bon voyage
and left to pack up my tent.

I felt rested. I felt organised. I felt ready to be back
in the wilds. Compared to much of the walk so far, the
initial going was easy. Like I was over the hump and on a
gentle incline coasting towards the end of the Cape Wrath
Trail. My pack was a little on the heavy side, what with the
resupply of food and wine, but my body didn't grumble.
It seemed I'd finally become trail fit, or maybe I had just
beaten my body into submission.

There were more incredible landscapes. More hills.
More lochs. More rivers. There was even a bit more
trackless pathless heather bashing over Bealach na Croise.
By this time I think I had become inured to both the
epicness of the scenery and the stubbornness of the
route. Around midday I plugged myself into my movie
soundtrack playlist. Trainspotting, Ferris Bueller's Day Off
and Guardians of the Galaxy amongst others. Again the

97

miles flowed underfoot.

After a hot chocolate and snack stop I almost left my walking poles behind. I walked all of two hundred yards before my hands and arms reminded me that there was something missing. It was only then that I turned around to look back at where I had been sitting that I noticed my sticks stuck in the ground where I'd left them. They kind of winked at me in the sunlight, daring me to continue without them. I hastily retrieved them and berated myself for my thoughtlessness.

I arrived at Shenavall Bothy in yet another stunning lochside glen and I was surprised to see a dozen people sunbathing outside. Maybe I'd burned up all my social etiquette the day before, but after a brief hello I left them to it and pitched my tent a few hundred metres away. I had just started cooking up my pasta and bean feast bolognese supper when a cloud decided that an impromptu shower was in order. This enhanced my anti-social feelings and sent the sunbathing bothy dwellers scurrying indoors.

At dinner the evening before I had spoken with a walker who was well and truly signed up to the fast and light ethos. In his quest to shave extra grammes from the overall weight that he carried, in place of a stove he had an empty plastic Skippy's peanut butter jar. He put dried noodles and water in this jar, and shook it vigorously. This rehydrated the noodles and made them just about edible. While I wasn't convinced the weight saving gain justified suffering cold noodles, it did dawn on me that I didn't need to simmer my dinner for 15 minutes as the pack suggested. I just needed to bring my food to the boil, put a lid on it, switched the gas off and let my dinner sit for

30 minutes. It took longer to cook my dinner but it meant I used much less gas. It also meant that there was less chance of carbon monoxide poisoning when sheltering from the rain in my tent. Every day's a school day, I reflected.

Kinlochewe Forest.

DAY 9

Shenavall to Loch an Daimh

Weather: Cloudy with the odd spot of rain and very little wind

21.3 miles, 1476 metres of ascent

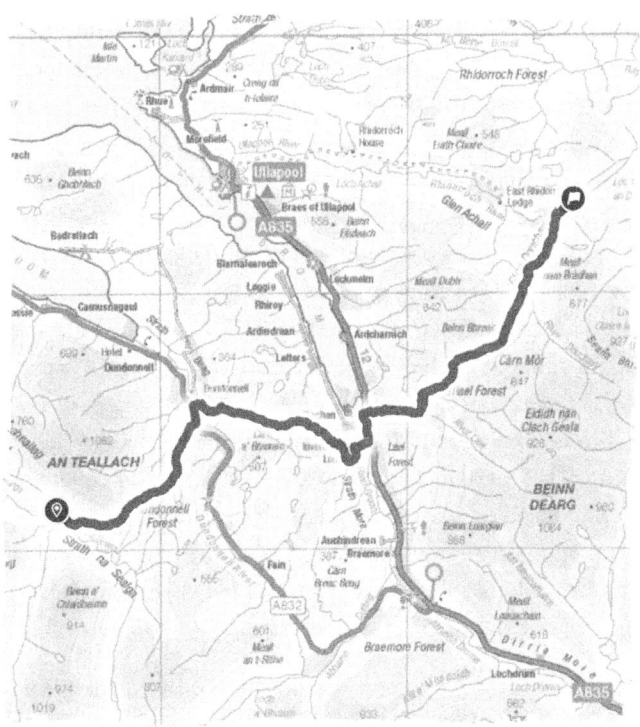

I slept well and was quietly in wonder at how my body had settled down to the abuse I was giving it. On the trail by 6.15am after a beautiful sunrise, I headed up out of the glen. With no wind, the morning felt incredibly still. It felt like time had been frozen.

Ahead of me was a day of ups and downs, both geographically and mentally. I crossed Dundonnell Forest, where there were not only no trees but no signs that there ever had been trees, and then I walked down to Corrie Hallie.

With nothing to detain me I ascended the second up of the day and briefly dallied by a waterfall for a hot chocolate and Snickers. Then it was down to Inverlael, crossing the highway that is the A835 with traffic flying up to Ullapool. I scurried away from the road and the scary cars like some startled wild thing. I headed up once more, this time traversing a commercial forest. With its maze of tracks I took a wrong turn. By the time I discovered that I wasn't where I should be, it would have required at least a mile of zig-zag backtracking to rectify. I opted for the direct approach and cut straight up through what looked like the morning after the day before of the Battle of the Ents. It was tree carnage. Navigation was easy enough, as all I had to do was head uphill until I hit the next track. The going was tough and precarious with the ground covered by woodland desolation. Ankle-snapping opportunities were high. Very carefully and with great deliberation on choosing where to place my feet, I made it to the correct forestry track and was back on route.

Once out of the forestry plantation I crossed Inverlael Forest which, like Dundonnell Forest, was not only devoid of trees but also had no evidence that there had ever been any trees. The landscape was typical Scottish moorland boggy heather, much like the stuff I'd been tramping across for over a week, so I can only assume that the forest label on the maps is historical. The sky had been moody all morning but it only managed to drop a dozen spots of rain on me. The clag had descended to shroud the hillsides across the way from where I was headed and I hoped it wasn't going to encroach further on my path, although technically there was no path. The next leg contoured around an unnamed hill and then down into Glen Douchary. It was another of the Cape Wrath Trail's "make-it-up-as-you-go-along" sections. Glen Douchary is fabled for its deep bogs and the guidebook described it as "a horrible mess that will destroy your spirits".

Blessed once more for experiencing such dry weather, I was let off lightly, although I remained ever vigilant and sought firm terra firma. Once over the bog factor, the guidebook describes Glen Douchary as stunningly beautiful with unique flora and fauna, but I found it a desolate location. Maybe it was the grey claggy day? Maybe the guidebook had been right after all about the place destroying your spirit? Maybe the miles were catching up with me?

Sometimes the membrane that separates my conscious from the subconscious, and reality from dreams, wears a little thin. This boundary typically becomes stretched and frayed in my life when I am physically/mentally stressed and/or sleep deprived. This state of mind is usually not welcome. On this walk, perhaps due to the solitude and physicality of romping through epic raw landscapes combined with my isolation within it, I had become much more emotionally sensitive. This had manifested itself with feelings of supercharged happiness and sheer unadulterated joy on more than one occasion. But slogging through the marshes of Glen Douchary, I was struck by an overwhelming melancholy. I missed my wife Jo. I missed my daughters Mia and Florence.

I wondered why I set myself such a punishing pace. Yes, I needed to lop a couple of days off my initial schedule to meet my retrieve driver and hit my work commitments. But at 19 days it had been a relaxed itinerary. When I arrived at Kinlochewe three days ahead of schedule I reasoned I should slow down and enjoy the adventure. I had joked with other Cape Wrath Trailers I met about the fast and light posse, questioning their motives and lamenting that they were missing so much of the beauty of the Highlands. I had also spoken to a fast/light chap who had been forced to give up due to injuries from the stress he had placed on his body. Yet here I was walking over 12 hours a day. Covering more miles and climbing more metres than my body should have been happy with. I told myself that it wasn't a race, or if it was a race, that it was only a race inside my head. The only person I was racing against was myself and there was always only going to be one winner and, more likely, one loser in that race. Yet once I had hit my pace and built up momentum, I found it impossible to slow down. I was treading a fine line between speed and failure. Looking back, I think I was driven by the desire to return to my family. And the only way to achieve that was to get to that lighthouse at the most northwestern tip of Scotland (or crash and burn and get the first train home!?!).

Checking my bearings on the map, my eye was drawn to the "Keep going!" card that Florence had made for me. I felt the ebb and flow of emotions shift, and a new resolve hardened within me. The melodic strains of "Welcome home, son," by Radical Face played through my headphones. I pulled my cloak of steely determination tight around me. Just "Keep going!" One foot in front of the other. Focus on the next step. And then the next. Don't lose yourself in contemplating the impossible task that still lay ahead. It would overwhelm me. All I had to do was take another step.

This may sound crazy (can it get any worse than my previous revelations?) but there were times when I felt that Jo, Mia and Florence were there with me, walking by my side. Before you reach for your phone to dial Social Services and get them to come and take me away, I do realise that my family were not physically with me. But I also knew for certain that in that moment they were willing me on.

My despondency passed and I was once more revelling in the landscape. Across the floor of the glen I joined a faint token of a path that followed the River Douchary. After trackless meanderings I found the path heartening. It represented a way that others had passed and their feet had trodden. The river had carved out a beautiful fairy-tale canyon dotted with waterfalls. I smiled at the prospect of disturbing some creature or other from Scottish folklore. My reverie was violently shattered as a lagopus lagopus scotica exploded from cover a foot from my feet. Involuntarily I let out one of those nervous laughs that are supposed to signal nonchalance but fool no one. "So much for Highland mythical creatures. Watch out for the red grouse!" I thought as I took a moment to regain my composure. With their rich chestnut plumage and distinctive red eyebrows, these birds had startled me more than once whilst I was hacking across heather-clad hills.

My little toe had become progressively painful. I'd irrationally been trying to ignore it. I couldn't quite believe that, after eight days of problem-free walking, now on the afternoon of the ninth day, I had developed a blister. It seemed most inconvenient to stop and remove my boot to inspect the itinerant toe. By the time I did stop to administer first aid, I had left it far too long. The ups, and more probably the downs, had caught up with me. I hastily taped up my foot and hobbled on.

An hour later at the head of Loch an Daimh I decided to call it a day. Knockdamph Bothy was less than a couple of miles further but the weather was fair and I preferred this idyllic wild camp shoreside location flanked by sublime hills. With the tent pitched, I sipped a medicinal brandy. Healing for both my body and spirit. Basking in the late afternoon sun in my own private corner of Scotland, half a dozen mountain bikers made their slow descent towards me from whence I had just come from. The ground I'd walked through had been incredibly rough and boggy. When they drew close, I joked with them that I would more likely be pushing my bike than riding it across such harsh terrain. They confided in me that that was exactly what they had done. Starting in Ullapool they had covered nine miles. Some of their party were looking pretty fed up, but they brightened when I mentioned they would soon connect with a good 4x4 track and their destination for the day, Knockdamph Bothy, wasn't far away.

River Douchary.

DAY 10

Loch an Daimh to Loch Ailsh

Weather: Started cloudy but soon became sunny and warm

20.1 miles, 532 metres of ascent

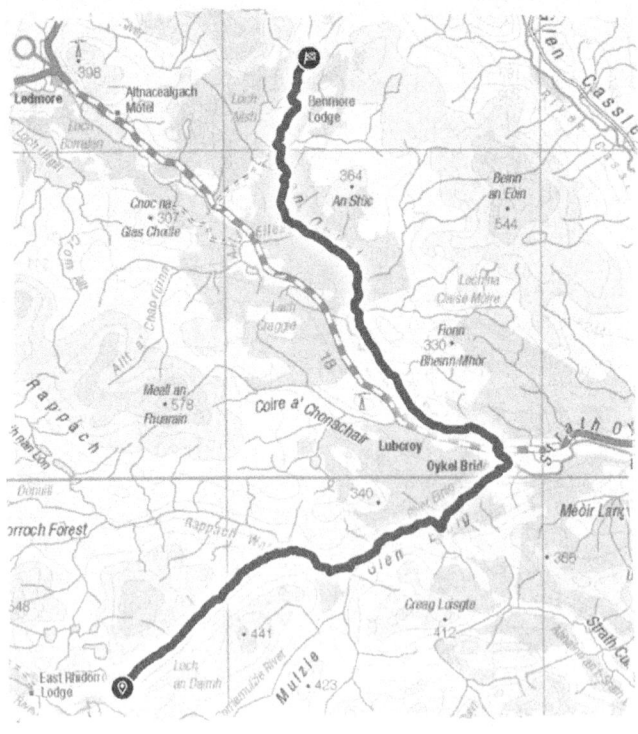

I was treated to another lovely sunrise as I packed my tent and made ready for the day ahead. I read in the guidebook that the going would be about as easy as it got, along 4x4 tracks. It was not to be the most thrilling of day's walking but I was grateful for the respite. My body ached and my toe was sore. As I hobbled the first few miles I wondered if I'd be able to complete the walk. Eventually my body loosened up and I did my best to ignore my throbbing foot.

Apart from the benefits of the distance, the remoteness and the jaw-dropping views, if you are into bagging bothies then this is the trail for you. The first bothy of day ten was Knockdamph, where its inhabitants of weary mountain bikers still slumbered. A logbook entry deadpanned, "Dead sheep in storage/workshop area at rear of bothy. Starting to go off a bit. Otherwise fine (the bothy, not the sheep)."

Not long after that I passed the Schoolhouse Bothy, which not surprisingly used to be a school. It served the local population up until 1930. A Northern Times report noted that the pupils' commute could be hazardous and that they often used stilts to cross the swollen River Einig to get to school. That was an inventive river crossing technique that had not occurred to me, although carrying stilts may have hindered me in other ways. Someone had made an entry in the bothy logbook claiming that their grandmother used to attend the school as a child. She had lived four miles further up the glen and knew a boy who came to school on the back of a pig and when it was time to go home the pig would be there to pick him up. I made a mental note to see if I could perhaps train a pig to facilitate my children's school run.

The morning I passed the Schoolhouse Bothy there was

no sign of any pigs but I did meet Lynne. She was a lovely optimistic person who had worked as an outdoor instructor until she was struck down with Lyme disease, a bacterial infection contracted from infected deer ticks. It is not that common in the UK, and because the symptoms of high temperature, headaches, muscle pain and lethargy are fairly general, it is often misdiagnosed. Early treatment is key to a swift recovery and unfortunately Lynne wasn't diagnosed for many months. It had taken her more than a year and a half to recover and she really struggled psychologically with not being able to get out into the hills that she loved. She was walking the Cape Wrath Trail in celebration of beating the illness and was revelling in being back out in her beloved playground. Lynne had been raised in the area and described this section of the Cape Wrath Trail as if she was coming home. She was meeting up with her family, who she hadn't seen for over two weeks, for lunch at Oykel Bridge, another five miles on. Her enthusiasm and joy for the great outdoors were infectious. With a broad grin I wished her the very best of luck with the rest of walk.

Oykel Bridge was also my destination for lunch. It actually boasted two bridges, an old bridge and a new one. The original bridge was built sometime in the 18th century and now services those travelling by shanks's pony, i.e. on foot. The newer bridge was built in the 1930s and affords the modern automobile safe passage across the river. Both are constructed by way of a magnificent single stone arch and are stunning pieces of civil engineering.

Of more importance to me was Oykel Bridge's single building, the Oykel Bridge Hotel, where I had high hopes of hearty nourishment. On arriving at 10.30am the place looked deserted and my hopes dwindled. Around the back I found a lady in an outbuilding laundering bedding. With little confidence I gingerly enquired if the hotel was open and if there was any chance of any food. She stopped what she was doing and was only too happy to show me to the guests' lobby at the front of the hotel. She explained that it was a changeover day, hence the lack of occupants, and because it was a Sunday the restaurant wouldn't be open until 12.30pm. I had lost track of the days of the week and was only really aware of how many days it had been since I had left Fort William because I had been keeping notes. My heart, or rather my stomach, sank as it thought that two hours sounded like a very long time to wait. Then the lady informed me that the kitchen could rustle up a bacon roll or a scone with jam and cream. My stomach did a triple somersault with joy and I said, "Yes, please." "Which would I like?" the lady asked. "Both, please!" was my (stomach's) instant reply. "And do you have tea and orange juice?" I asked. She apologised that the orange juice wouldn't be freshly squeezed, but I reassured her that it wasn't a problem.

I will be constantly amazed by the warm hospitality that well-to-do establishments like the Oykel Bridge Hotel offer to the humble walker. The lady seemed oblivious of my dishevelled and somewhat fragrant state. Whilst waiting in the empty guest lounge I took the opportunity to remove my boots, checked for ticks and checked my progress on my maps. I noted that I was on map square 32 of 44. The end of the walk was now much closer than the beginning. I briefly allowed myself to believe that there was a real possibility of making it to Cape Wrath. A heavily burdened tray arrived with a feast upon it and my attention snapped immediately back to the present. With great restraint, I took a photo before devouring the contents. It was delicious.

With a gap nicely filled and approaching midday I asked the lady who came to clear my empty pots away when and where they would like me for lunch. I had learned from the Kinlochewe Hotel debacle not to take anything for granted. She took my order and showed me to the dining room. Again this was completely deserted and I had the place to myself. A few moments later she returned and sheepishly asked if I wouldn't mind moving to the bar snug as they wanted to set the tables in the restaurant for evening service. I reassured her that I'd be happy to eat in the car park if that was where the food would be served.

It might have been the bacon roll and scone starter or that a Sunday roast is one of my favourite meals that I have refined and perfected over the years in my own kitchen, but the Oykel Bridge Sunday roast wasn't the greatest that I had ever eaten. Not that I left a single morsel on my plate. However, the bottle of house red was more than palatable, although still being early afternoon with a few more miles ahead of me I surreptitiously decanted the half bottle I didn't drink into the plastic bottles I carried for later. Feeling rather sated I paid the bill and moseyed on.

Not long after leaving the hotel I met Lynne again. She was with her family enjoying a feast of a picnic on the original Oykel Bridge. She greeted me like an old friend, as did her family. They asked if I would like to join them but I explained that I was stuffed and probably could do with a walk. They felt bad that they couldn't give me anything, so more out of obligation than necessity I accepted a couple of clementines. Once again I wished Lynne the best of luck with the rest of her journey. Like so many chance encounters I knew it was unlikely our paths would cross again, but I felt enriched by the experience of meeting a like-minded person and sharing a moment of kinship.

The rest of the afternoon's walking was along the banks of the River Oykel on well-maintained tracks that existed to drop off well-heeled folk at the various fishing beats. Salmon fishing season on the River Oykel was from May to September. Fishing is by traditional fly only and strict conservation rules have been in place for many years. Apparently the best beats are booked up many years in advance. Again my timing was immaculate, and being too early for fishing I had the place to myself. I took full advantage of the regularly well-placed benches to rest and brew up a cup of tea. The going was steady, bordering on boring, but as I had a very full stomach I was grateful for the relief from hacking across steep, trackless, rough hills. The blister I'd taped up the previous day continued to throb uncomfortably.

By late afternoon just beyond where the River Oykel flowed into Loch Ailsh I found yet another idyllic camp spot. If you've read this far and paid attention, you will have come to realise that almost anywhere in the Highlands is an idyllic wild campsite. This one was just off the beaten track in a tucked-away location sheltered by a stand of pines next to a minor meandering tributary with swallows performing an aerial ballet above my head. Being sheltered and next to a stream it would probably be hell in midge season. That evening I lounged outside my tent cooking dinner and making notes whilst the sun went down. I could see midges about, and I applied some Smidge, but they were nowhere near as voracious as I had previously experienced. I can only guess that the unaccustomed dryness coupled with the time of year meant that their numbers had been severely affected. I didn't have any complaints.

As for my throbbing blistered toe I decided that action was required. Deploying a surgical scalpel blade I made a surgical strike. Piercing and draining the blister I felt instant relief. I know there are pros and cons to this approach. Potentially I was opening my toe up to infection, but my Swann Morton scalpel blades are made for surgeons and are about as sterile as it gets. If they are good enough for the world's elite surgeons to perform open-heart surgery, they are good enough for me. Being a graphic designer I have used them for the more prosaic task of making mock-ups. I have read that some ultra-marathon athletes leave a strand of cotton threaded through the blister so it doesn't seal up, thus allowing it to drain. I wasn't quite that extreme, and once I had drained all the fluid I applied compeed, a plaster that mimics skin. My surgery was done for the day.

Oykel Bridge.

DAY 11

Loch Ailsh to Glendhu Bothy

Weather: Cool morning then warm and sunny. The wind increased throughout the day.

22 miles, 1416 metres of ascent

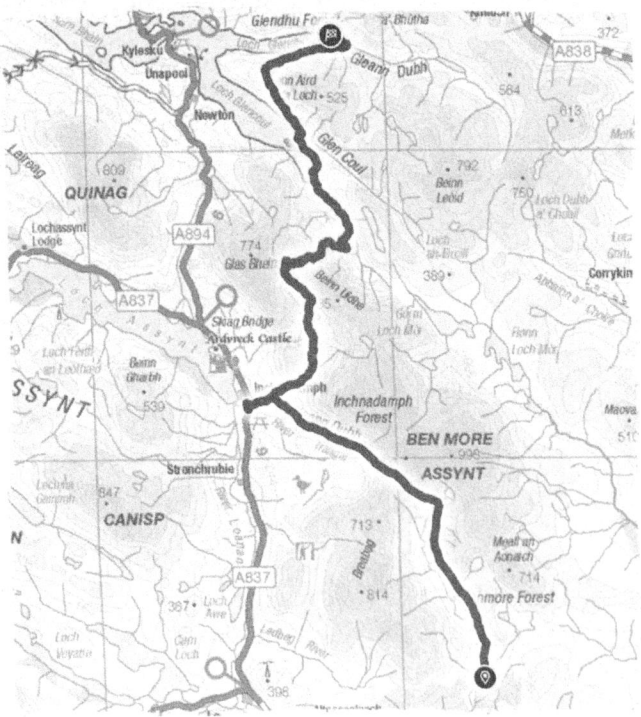

Over breakfast I was treated to another extraordinary sunrise (yawn!). I really enjoyed the early mornings that my walking routine afforded. I found it spellbinding to watch the world slowly awake. Adding to the enchantment, the dawn light glimmered off a thin layer of mist suspended above the loch.

Once I'd downed my morning Ready Brek I decided to pre-empt a day of pain by taking a couple of ibuprofen tablets. I had been reluctant to take painkillers and this was the first time since leaving Fort William that I had succumbed. This was not because I was of the opinion that my body was a temple, but because I reasoned that it would be wise to tune in and listen to my body and so avoid potential problems. This strategy had failed, and after the previous day of general physical whingeing and my foot screaming at me, "I hurt!" I decided enough was enough and it was time to apply some metaphorical earplugs. I redesignated my body's status from temple to pharmaceutical theme park and felt much better for it.

I was now ensconced in Assynt territory. I had been surprised to notice the subtle differences in Highland terrain as I journeyed north. Knoydart was green and Wester Ross craggy. In the upper reaches of Glen Oykel the hills were covered in yellow-brown heather. The rough track faded away and the liberating, but slightly intimidating, feeling of remoteness enveloped me. Cloud hung low on the hills and obscured the way. Approaching cloud base I became concerned about navigation through the murk. I could see on the map where I was heading, but on the ground, with no path and impending clag, visual clues were all but hidden. I distracted myself by throwing a few silly shadow shapes across the hillside in the low morning sunlight. I needn't have worried, and as I ascended the valley between Ben More Assynt and Breabag, like a well-choreographed performance, the cloud lifted to reveal the bealach. I celebrated with a hot chocolate in glorious sunshine.

The way down wasn't clear but not due to cloud. The obvious route following Allt a' Bhealaich soon disappeared into a steep ravine. Once again ViewRanger kept me on track, and I counter intuitively ascended further and contoured around Conival before dropping down to follow the River Traligill. I passed a couple of walkers heading up in the direction that I had just come from. This was my first human encounter since leaving Oykel Bridge the previous day. The chap was sporting a day-glo yellow jacket which made me want to don my sunglasses. We stopped for a short chat as is customary when walking in the hills. They were from the Netherlands and regularly came on holiday to the Highlands. Wishing them well I headed down to Inchnadamph.

Inchnadamph Hotel was the location which hopefully had my third and final supply parcel and perhaps even a room for the night if their rates weren't too steep. First of all, I passed a lodge and I thought it would be wise to check out my options. Graham, the proprietor, gave me a warm welcome, a cup of tea on the house and free access to their wifi. Asking about accommodation he showed me a choice of a dorm bed or a private room. Unfortunately he didn't allow camping but he told me about a place a few hundred yards away where I could wild camp. I explained that I had sent a supply parcel to the hotel and that I hoped to avail myself of the restaurant. Graham explained that the hotel, including the restaurant, was closed except for private functions. He added that if I had no luck there I could buy one of lodge's ready meals and use the hostel's kitchen facilities. I thanked him and headed to the hotel.

The hotel was uncommonly quiet as I entered and rang the bell on the reception desk. A few minutes later a chap appeared. I explained that I had sent a supply parcel and asked if it had arrived. The fellow, obliging, retrieved the familiar box from behind the reception. I thanked him and asked about the possibility of a room. Alas, he was closed for a private function. "And the restaurant?" I enquired. Also closed. "What about the bar?" Nope, closed. Oh, well. I thanked him for holding onto my food parcel and headed back to the lodge.

Graham was good to his word and opened up his freezer, revealing an icy Aladdin's cave of ready meals. I opted for a fish pie and a pepperoni pizza. The height of fine dining sophistication if you had just spent 10 days in the wilds of the Scottish Highlands. Whilst lunch was cooking I repacked my bag, assimilating my new supplies and discarding anything I didn't need. I also took advantage of the lodge's large dining table to lay out my remaining map squares end to end. It then dawned on me that if I pressed on I could possibly get to Cape Wrath within another two days, although this did heavily depend on me being able to safely cross the bombing range. I could barely believe I was so close to my goal.

With lunch munched and a dessert of a couple more ibuprofen tablets, I thanked Graham for his hospitality and headed out the door. The guidebook described the next stage as one of the hardest, but finest, of the whole trail and recommended at least a day to cover it. I was starting it at 2 o'clock in the afternoon. I was slowly coming to terms with being driven and had given up fighting it. I was no good at slowing down and pacing myself, so I embraced what was. Besides, after a grand gourmet lunch, and as the painkillers kicked in, I felt energised and ready to walk. It was what I had come here to do. Cape Wrath beckoned and I could not resist its call. The guidebook intoned that I would be entering some of the best mountain country in the world, but I had stopped listening to the guidebook and was now following my heart.

I plugged myself into a playlist and hurled myself back into Assynt. The terrain was glorious. If you have read this far you are probably becoming jaded with my constant use of the words "beautiful", "amazing", "awesome" and "jaw-dropping". As an amateur wordsmith I completely fail to conjure the majesty of what I was experiencing. I challenge anyone to do justice to the Highland landscape using the hopelessly inadequate medium of words. Magnificent? Breathtaking? Astonishing? Still hopelessly deficient in even getting close to describing the country I was floating through.

The afternoon weather was kind to the point of divine. Blue skies dotted with friendly cumulus. And a light cooling breeze. The pathfinding was effortless even towards the top of Bealach na h-Uidhe where the track petered out. The terrain under foot could have been austere, but with the day I had it was a joy to hopscotch from rock to rock. I was taken back to a childhood seaside summer holiday.

Carefree and left to my own devices, out of sight of my parents, innocent and oblivious to potential consequences, I danced from giant rock to giant rock along a harbour breakwater.

When I crested the bealach I was forced to take a seat. Not through tiredness but with what was before me. I had crossed many passes and seen some truly epic landscapes but at the top of Bealach na h-Uidhe I struck Highland gold. The expanse was huge. Mountain after raw rocky mountain ranged from horizon to horizon. I stopped trying to comprehend my route through it all and accepted my insignificance within it. I laughed aloud and danced. The crescendo of Salva Mea by Faithless was my soundtrack of that moment. I took a long pause, gulping in air, absorbing the occasion.

Steadying myself I headed down into the unfolding landscape with a new-born self-belief. Reliving my former innocent, fearless, younger self, gambolling across the rocks, I was completely unafraid. Whilst I may be meaningless in this land, this land held meaning to me. I was exactly where I should be. The moment of that refined rarefied time and space resonated with some deeply buried chord within me.

Alas, or maybe fortunately, such states of mind and feelings of emotion cannot be sustained. I enjoyed a short-lived frolic around a few lochans before plummeting down to the river that flowed into Loch Beag at the end of a sea loch. Once in the steep-sided valley following the river I found the going tough and trackless. The euphoria of being up high became a distant memory. Back to the task at hand, my feet functioned mechanically and plodded on.

With hindsight I am able to see how close some of the highs are to some of the lows. This isn't a complaint. It is an observation and maybe a reflection of the mental state induced by long distance walking. Who knows?

Eventually the sharpness of the mountain corridor opened out as I approached Loch Glencoul and the picturesque location for another bothy. It was 7pm and apart from a fair lick of wind it could not have been a more perfect evening. I probably should have stopped at Glencoul Bothy for the night but I think the heady scent of Cape Wrath not much beyond my grasp pushed me on. So I found myself turning my back on this prime location and heading up and over the next headland. The evening light was hypnotic, and just as I had that morning when walking up Glen Oykel, which felt a millennia ago, I threw a few shadow shapes across the heather.

As the light was fading and exhaustion was catching up with me I rounded Loch Glendhu and approached Glendhu Bothy. In the evening dusk the wind was approaching hooleying levels as I entered the building. At just before 9pm, with 14 hours' walking beneath my boots and seven hours since lunch, I was proper tired and hungry. I met, and briefly introduced myself to, Angie, the sole occupant of the bothy – a German lady in her sixties who was also walking the Cape Wrath Trail. To this day I feel some guilt, as I wasn't as polite or friendly as I should have been. I apologised for my late intrusion and brusquely stated I was hungry and needed to sort out dinner. After relatively brisk introductions she said she was away to bed as she was having an early start in the morning. In the dimming light I set about brewing a tea and snaffling a

Snickers as my mac cheese simmered. Luckily there were two sleeping rooms so I didn't disturb Angie as I went up to bed.

The River Oykel with Ben More Assynt in early morning cloud.

The view from the top of Bealach na h-Uidhe.

Hello Scotland!

DAY 12

Glendhu Bothy to Rhiconich

Weather: Blue skies and hot

19.2 miles, 995 metres of ascent

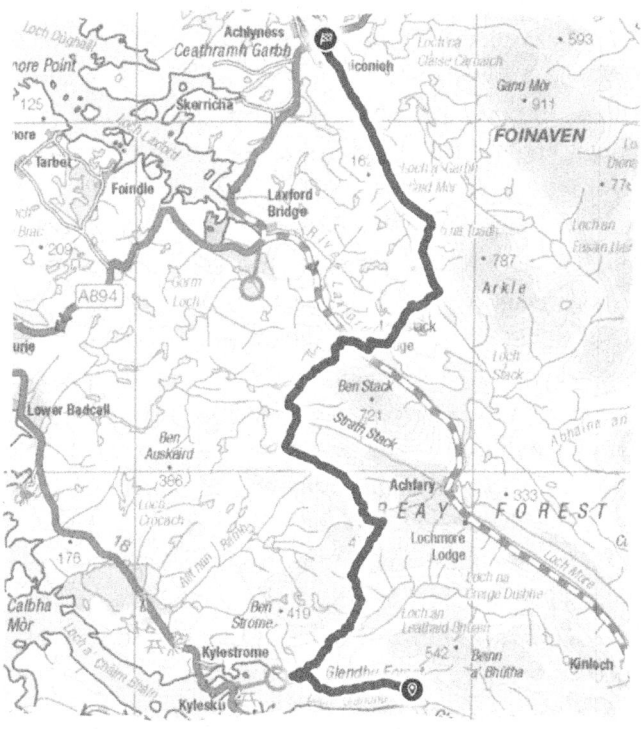

Perhaps it was due to being serenaded by the King of Hoolies and his council, Queen Gale and Lord Gusty, but I did not sleep well. I was vaguely grateful that I was not in my tent at 4.30am when I gave up the pretence of sleep and ate my Ready Brek. At the very least the bothy offered shelter for cooking; however, the building seemed to amplify the noise of the wind outside.

The day dawned, clear blue skies were revealed and I was in for more unseasonably hot Highland strolling. I started slowly walking west by the shores of the loch on an easygoing 4x4 track. My body limbered up, my new regime of compeed and ibuprofen silencing my feet. The guidebook suggested that to reach Rhiconich in a day would be challenging even for the fittest walkers. Although the mileage wasn't excessive, the terrain would be rough, with significant trackless sections. "Business as usual," I thought to myself. I also concluded that I must reappraise how I see myself as a walker. I don't believe I'm particularly fit or even much of an experienced gnarly outdoors type. You may perceive this as false modesty but in my mind I'm an average Joe. Yes, I have done some walking but I regularly make mistakes and find myself beyond my comfort zone. I generally survive due to my stubbornness to keep going and my refusal to give up. Throughout the Cape Wrath Trail I had been regularly covering distances that Iain Harper's guidebook suggested should take longer and be much more difficult. Again I appreciated how fortunate I had been with the weather and how much easier it had made my journey. I still refused to accept that I'm some kind of Highland athlete. The mere thought of that was enough to make me laugh out loud.

To try and aid pacing I made a conscious effort to stop every hour or two. The beautiful weather expedited many tea breaks. I had neglected my evening routine of note-taking the previous day, as I had been tired and the daylight had run out. I decided to shake things up a bit and got a little radical. Instead of waiting to the evening I now dug out my pen and paper to scrawl down whatever meandering thoughts were running through my head whenever I stopped. This new strategy had twin benefits. The first was that I recorded more before I forgot what I had been pondering, which often happened with my goldfish-like memory. The second plus was that I took longer rest breaks. I had always struggled to sit still, even with the stunning vistas to absorb. As soon as I had come up with my new cutting-edge note-taking habit, my one and only pen ran out. I cursed it silently and wondered where I might find a new pen in this distant part of the world.

The walking was for the most part straightforward, across rolling country. The only bealach of the day was a rather humble affair of less than 400 metres. Even when the route took me over the top of a hill, I barely registered it. The Cape Wrath Trail for the most part avoided summits, but I think, as this stretch had a minimal amount of ups, Iain Harper decided to add in a few extra just for fun. Mind you, Ben Dreavie, at 503 metres, was lower than many of the bealachs I had crossed.

Dropping down to Feur Lochan my focus wandered and I stepped into a bog. Both legs up to the knees. For the first time since starting the walk. I extricated myself as quickly as I had gone in and escaped with dry feet. I thanked my gaiters for their good service and weighed my complacency critically.

I hadn't seen another person all day or any signs of civilisation, so when I came to the A838 it was a bit of a shock. This particular stretch of road was fairly straight and the intermittent passing traffic thundered down it at frightening speeds. I surveyed it suspiciously from afar, perhaps like early man had first viewed fire's destructive flames. I did not enjoy the 200 metres of road walking and practically ran the distance to where a driveway turned off to Stack Lodge.

Stack Lodge is quite a grand country house. I noticed a couple of joiners building a new porch and approached them. Perhaps it was because I was out of practice at conversing with people (I had become well practised at conversing with the local flora and fauna!), but I began to babble a little wildly. I started by asking them for a huge favour then I explained that I was walking the Cape Wrath Trail and had started in Fort William many days ago and was in a spot of bother. Both tradesmen's faces were a picture of worried puzzlement, uncertain of where I was headed with my request. Finally I told them that I had been keeping a diary and that my pen had run out. "Oh, so you would like a pen?" the gaffer asked with palpable relief in his voice. "Yes, please," I confirmed, "and I'll pay whatever you ask for one!" I added. He laughed, saying that a good story was more than enough payment and after rooting around his van's dashboard triumphantly handed me a biro. For good measure he also plucked a pencil from behind his ear and passed it to me announcing that it wouldn't run out of ink. I thanked him profusely and went on my way.

The afternoon was hot and I stopped frequently to drink water from burns and lochs I passed. I had an extended lunch break eating cheddar and chorizo, washed down with Scotland's finest H2O in the shadow of the magnificent Arkle mountain. Deploying my newly acquired writing instruments I did my best to capture the last 48 hours' thoughts and happenings as they flowed from my consciousness.

Garbh Allt feeding into Loch a' Garbh-bhaid Mòr presented me with a surprise challenge. I had become laissez faire towards the river crossings, but despite the dry weather this one wasn't going to be easy. Although not particularly fast flowing, there was a reasonable stretch of water to cross. I thought about deploying my as yet unused trail shoes but decided to follow the river upstream. A noticeable path had formed where others had also gone in search of an easier crossing. Half a mile up from the loch, where a small stream joined the river, I found a string of rocks across the water and decided that they offered my best chance of dry feet. It wasn't ideal, and even with my walking poles aiding my balance I slipped and plunged one foot into the drink. With a desperate leap I vaulted to the far bank saving myself a prolonged foot bath. I dread to think what that river crossing would have been like in more customary Scottish weather.

The rest of the afternoon passed mostly uneventfully. Walking the last few miles to Rhiconich along the banks of the loch, I heard a droning noise and located a couple of Hercules planes trundling up the glen hugging the ridge. Flying less than 50 metres above the ground at a ponderous rate it took a while for them to pass. My thoughts turned to the Cape Wrath bombing range where these planes were undoubtedly returning from. I wondered if I would have several days enforced rest in Kinlochbervie whilst the MOD finished playing their games. An unwelcome pause so close to goal was not a pleasant prospect.

The hotel in Rhiconich, however, was a pleasant prospect with the promise of proper food and red wine. It is superbly located at the head of Loch Inchard and has great views. I arrived at 4.30pm and discovered that the bar opened an hour later and the kitchen another hour after that. I scoped out a camp spot on the beach of the loch and then brewed up a hot chocolate at one of the hotel's outside tables. Bang on 5.30pm the doors opened and I was their first customer at the bar.

I relaxed enjoying the luxurious delights of a wine from a glass whilst sitting on a chair, with the lighthouse potentially only a day away. Brian, another Cape Wrath Trailer (you can spot them a mile off), arrived at the hotel bar. He had a room booked and was aiming to finish the walk in a couple of days. We shared our experiences of the trail and I found out he had been an engineer in the army. Although he had left the forces over a decade earlier, he claimed to have connections who were in the know about the Cape Wrath bombing range and the current operations underway. He seemed optimistic about our chances of a safe crossing. I hoped his information was good. We finished our meals and he headed off to bed. I prepared to retreat to my camp ground. Settling the bill at the bar, the landlady suggested a good place was next to the police station and a little beyond Rhiconich's public toilets. I voiced my reservations about practically sleeping in the back garden of the police station and she assured me that it was only used once a fortnight. I thanked her and left.

It turned out to be a perfect spot on a flat patch of manicured grass. Its elevated position offered long-reaching views out over the sea loch and the public toilets meant I had en-suite facilities. Removing my boots I noticed that half the rubber toe protector was missing from the left one, probably the victim of my botched river crossing earlier that afternoon. The boots were only 14 months old. I had bought them after discovering the preceding pair were no longer watertight on a snowy walk. That had been exactly one month before I had departed on my last walk, the Southern Upland Way, at the end of March 2018. My current boots were now looking in a very sad state. The uppers were battered and the tread was beginning to resemble slicks on a Formula One car. With getting through a pair of boots in a little over a year, this walking pastime of mine was becoming expensive.

Loch Glendhu.

Arkle mountain.

DAY 13

Rhiconich to the Cape Wrath lighthouse

Weather: Overcast with occasional sun and a moderate breeze

20.5 miles, 786 metres of ascent

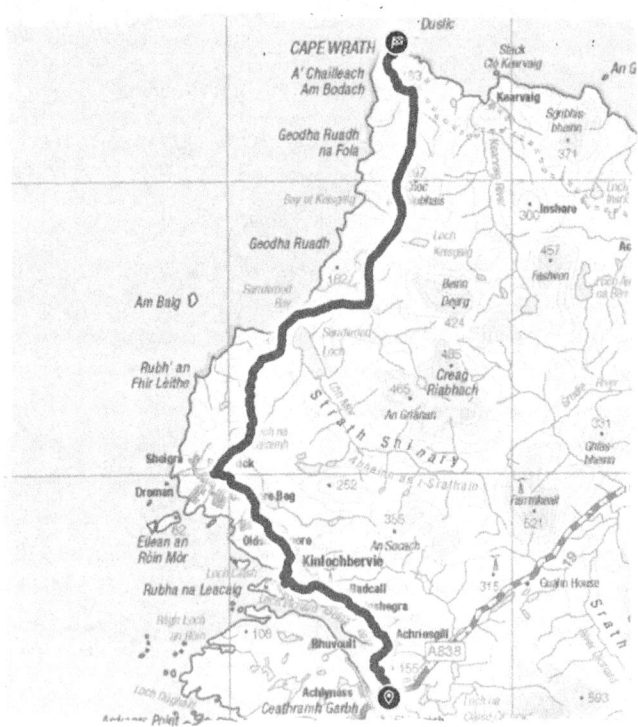

I woke at 5am with a mixture of excitement, anticipation and nerves. I forced myself to slow down. I wanted to pick up a couple of provisions from the Spar in Kinlochbervie. It didn't open until 9am and was only a couple of hours of road walking away. I boiled water for my breakfast and wondered whether the MOD were still bombing the small patch of Scotland that lay between me and my goal.

Using a proper toilet for my morning ablutions made a pleasant change from my usual routine and removed the necessity to dig a hole. All packed up I started the familiar shuffling, hobbling first steps of the day. Half way to Kinlochbervie I passed the Old School House B&B and café. A blackboard on the grass verge announced it was open for breakfast so I headed inside. I was welcomed, and a lady confirmed that it wasn't a mirage, a trick by my mind, and yes, a full Scottish breakfast was on offer. It was delicious and I used the last of my toast to wipe my plate clean. Feeling fortified and quite full from my second breakfast of the day I waddled on down the road.

A little further I passed through Badcall. Not a judgement on my decision making but the unfortunate name of a hamlet and the home of a shop called London Stores. This shop holds legendary status on the Cape Wrath Trail for stocking everything under the sun. I couldn't resist and popped in to have a nose around. Not much bigger than a single garage, the place was crammed floor to ceiling with goods. I came away with three postcards with a photo of a certain lighthouse on them.

At around 10am I wound my way down to the port town of Kinlochbervie. The place was more port than town, with a substantial harbour and only a few dozen houses. I liberated some bread, salami and a bottle of wine from the Spar. I wondered if I'd be drinking the wine in celebration of completing the walk at the lighthouse or drinking it killing time in a bus shelter in the company of the local yoofs, waiting for the firing range to open. It was time to find out, so I dug out the number for the range control and dialled. I wasn't optimistic, as various A4 signs had been posted in shops along the past few miles stating that military exercises would be continuing into May. A familiar, efficient, clear, clipped voice answered. Babbling slightly excitedly I explained that I was walking the Cape Wrath Trail and was in Kinlochbervie, and was there any chance of crossing the bombing range either that evening or in the morning without getting blown up, please? He took my jabbering in his stride and informed me that the range would be inactive from 7pm but in all likeliness exercises would finish much earlier that day. They would then resume at 5am the following morning. I felt like I had just been told that I had won the lottery. I could make the Cape Wrath lighthouse that day. Overjoyed I fist pumped the air, then sheepishly checked around to see if anyone was watching me. Fortunately there wasn't. Taking a deep breath I asked the MOD chap to repeat the information for clarity as it was not something you would want to misunderstand. I had heard the information correctly the first time. My spirits soared. I dared to believe that I might actually finish this walk and complete the challenge I had set myself just under a year ago.

With renewed vigour and a buoyancy in my step that my beleaguered feet should not have possessed, I picked up the signposted road to Sandwood Bay. With eight miles of easy but dull road walking ahead of me, I plugged myself into my tunes and strode out. In anticipation of finishing, and to fill the time, I composed a Cape Wrath Trail Oscar acceptance speech to deliver to the seagulls at the lighthouse...

"I've made it! I'm at the Cape Wrath lighthouse, the most northwesterly tip of mainland Britain. Closer to Iceland than London. I can't quite believe I'm here...

I would like to say a few 'thank yous'...

Firstly, thank you to you, yes YOU! My friends and family for taking an interest and for your words of encouragement.

Thank you to my wife Jo, and my children Mia and Florence, not only for allowing me to do this but also for your wholehearted support. For driving me up to Fort William and for seeing me off the ferry. Without that help I may well have disappeared into the first pub I came to, not to be seen again for two weeks.

Thank you to my brother-in-law, David, who drove all the way to Durness to catch me at the end of the trail and take me safely back home to West Yorkshire. If he had not met me, I may well have kept going, and it gets very wet after the Cape Wrath lighthouse.

I would like to thank my knees for not packing in on the second day. It was a near thing and probably the closest I got to not finishing the Cape Wrath Trail.

And finally I would like to thank my feet for all the abuse they have taken. Half a million steps across Scottish bogs and hills... oh, wait a minute, my feet have just told me that they would like to speak for themselves… they would like it on the record that they have been duped, hoodwinked and deceived. Spending two weeks in a dark confined space smelling aromatically of leather and cheese, whilst regularly getting water boarded in Highland bogs, is not their idea of a holiday and they will be writing a stiff letter of complaint to Amnesty International just as soon as the blisters have healed…"

Actually, my feet were complaining. The throbbing pain snapped me out of my musings and back to reality. I hadn't finished the walk yet and perhaps I was getting a little ahead of myself. I paused to top up on ibuprofen and my protesting feet quietened down.

I arrived at Sandwood Bay early in the afternoon. It is a special place, even among the many stunning beaches that dot the storm-lashed western coast of Scotland. There is something about it that makes it curiously atmospheric and compelling. A vast sweeping sand beach with perfect sets of waves rolling in from the North Atlantic. A naturally sculpted sea stack just off the coast framed the southern end and somewhere to the north on the hazy towering sea cliffs was the Cape Wrath lighthouse. The clouds briefly cleared to reveal pale blue sky as I walked along the sand, and deep azure North Atlantic sea glinted all the way to the horizon.

Sandwood Bay is an obvious camping place before the final push to the end of the trail in the morning. However, due to the MOD's timetable and my inner drive, I only allowed myself to stop long enough for a tea. After 20 minutes of absorbing the spectacular seascape and savouring its wild essence, I shouldered my pack, waved goodbye and climbed up out of the bay.

I only had eight more miles to go, but Iain Harper ominously warns that they can feel like the toughest miles of the whole trail. Completely trackless across beautiful but bleak peat-hag moors. I knew I had time to take it easy so wasn't too concerned. My bigger worry was getting to the bombing range's boundary too early and having to wait hours for the allotted safe time to cross.

I soon came to Strathchailleach Bothy, which has an interesting history. For over 30 years it was home to James McRory Smith aka Sandy. With no power, running water or telephone he lived the life of a Highland hermit, making the occasional trip to London Stores in Badcall to collect his pension and stock up on supplies. His paintings can still be seen on the bothy walls. From half a mile out I could see someone standing outside in a bright red top. By the time I got to the bothy the person had retreated inside and I was greeted by a very excited hound. I talked soothingly to her whilst she gave me a thorough sniffing. I must have met with her approval as she soon calmed down. The mystery person turned out to be an MBA MO (Mountain Bothy Association Maintenance Officer). Unusually, at least in my limited experience, she was a young woman. As it turned out she wasn't this bothy's MO but was there with the Strathchailleach Bothy's MO who was, as is more usual, an elderly gentleman. They were there to check the building over and cut some peat to dry out for fuel for the fire.

They both made me feel very welcome and boiled up a brew. The chap said that if peat cutting was on my bucket list then now was my chance and I was welcome to join them. I may have passed up an opportunity of a lifetime but declined the offer, explaining that peat cutting wasn't even on my outer radar let alone my bucket list. I thanked him for the opportunity to learn new skills and thanked them both for the time and energy that they and the other MBA volunteers put into maintaining the valuable resource of open shelters that are free for all to use.

As promised, there were no paths to follow but the moors didn't feel particularly bleak. The going was rough but fairly easy, because instead of being a boggy morass from hell the ground was only slightly damp and springy underfoot. I did try to slow down and enjoy the views but the invisible force that had been propelling me northwards for the past two weeks seemed to be pulling me stronger than ever. At 4.45pm, two and a quarter hours before the range was officially safe to cross, I reached the wire fence that delineated the boundary between safe ground and certain death. Prophetic red flags were fluttering at the top of the flagpoles dotted along the fence line. Just to underline the message, signs read: "Keep out when red flags are flying". Another sign declared bluntly that military debris may explode and kill me.

I'm not a patient person. I'd had enough tea breaks. I wanted to get this thing done. I questioned if it was safe to cross before the allotted time. Recalling my morning phone call, the MOD bloke had said he thought they would be finished long before the official 7pm time. I wondered if his idea of a long time was more or less than two and a quarter hours. The Hercules I had seen the day before had been flying home at 4pm. Gazing apprehensively across the terrain ahead, weighing up my chances, I noticed a herd of red deer on the brow of a hill in the distance. I took it as a good omen and reasoned that they wouldn't be hanging around if bombs were falling from the sky. Hesitantly I climbed the fence wondering if this was the most stupid thing I had ever done (and there was some stiff competition on that front!). Would my tombstone read "Here lies Will, who almost completed the Cape Wrath Trail"?

My ears strained for the fateful hum of aircraft engines or the screeching wine of a shell being hurled at me from a naval battleship stationed far out to sea. Nervous tension was a woefully inadequate description of my mental state. With my nerves jangling I eyed each peat-hag shelf I passed as a possible air raid shelter. My potential sudden demise gave me wings and I completely forgot about my complaining feet and limbs. My pace doubled. Halfway across the range and approaching 6.30pm without incident, I slowly began to relax believing I was probably safe.

For some time I had likened walking the Cape Wrath Trail to a game. The goal was to get from A to B. From Fort William to Cape Wrath. I moved by steps. Many steps are required but each individual step was a turn in the game. With each step I was trying to get closer to the finish but with each step there was risk involved, usually in the form of bogs and boulders. To play the game well it was paramount that I placed each foot with careful consideration, as securely as possible, and this took concentration. When crossing bogs I was focused on finding firm ground. I had become an expert on the Highland flora. I didn't know the names of the myriad of plant life I encountered but I knew their properties.

The ones which loved wet environments and will suck
you down into their spongy depths. And conversely I
recognised the plants that may provide a firmer foothold, a
vegetative stepping stone across the bog land. On rubble-
strewn hillsides it was about judging how solid a rock is.
Will it wobble? Is it slippery? Likewise when I was crossing
rivers. I thought I had become quite good at the game
but it takes a great deal of focus. If my chosen footfalls
are 99.9% well picked and there are 2000 steps in a mile,
statistics informs me that I would slip, trip or stumble
twice every mile. Definitely more when I was tired but
fortunately less when I was super focused. This could
mean something or nothing as I usually caught myself.
It could mean a wet foot which will increase my chance
of developing blisters. More seriously it could lead to a
twisted ankle or a snapped leg. Critically, it could result
in being pitched forward off a steep hillside into a deep
ravine. And that would be game over. So whilst I compared
it to a game, I was aware it was a very serious game with
potentially serious consequences.

I started to realise that I was going to complete the
Cape Wrath Trail and finish the game. The end had always
seemed so far off but now it was within my grasp. Before,
to even contemplate success, I felt I would be courting
disaster. A thunderbolt from the heavens? A meteorite
on its fateful path through space? A cartoon grand piano
falling from the sky? I was only a few hundred yards from
the 4x4 track that would take me to the lighthouse less
than a mile away.

It was at that moment that I suddenly and quite
unexpectedly found myself waist deep in bog after a

momentary lapse in concentration. One poorly judged footstep. I threw myself forward onto my stomach to spread my weight as best I could across the quagmire. I was aware that my feet were a good metre beneath the surface and still had no hint of purchase on anything solid. Throwing my walking poles ahead of me, I grabbed the nearby marsh grass and heaved myself to terra firma. Once out I rolled onto my back and hurled expletives at the sky. As my children may one day read this report I shall have to leave it to your own imagination as to the actual words I used.

This wasn't an earthy peat bog I had stumbled into. It was a stinking slimy green bog of the worst kind. I couldn't believe that I had travelled nearly 240 miles without even one wet foot. Now I was drenched up to the waist in fetored goo. Once over the initial shock I wondered if it was the Cape Wrath Trail giving me a giant, wet farewell kiss as a parting gesture.

There was a mile to go and I still had not seen the lighthouse. I hoped I hadn't misread the map. I hoped that some cosmic joke at my expense was not at play and that I had not ended up entirely in the wrong corner of Scotland. When I rounded a bend and saw the lighthouse as bold as brass not more than 400 yards away, I let out a cry of joy. Maybe it was a cry of relief?

Arriving at the lighthouse I wasn't overcome by euphoric elation as I had anticipated but by an overwhelming pressing need to shed my wet stinking clothes and exchange them for dry and warm attire. I had read that there was a bloke called John who ran an enterprise called the Ozone Café at Cape Wrath, allegedly open 24 hours, 7 days a week, aided by a pack of cocker spaniels. He was apparently always ready with a hot cup of tea and a plate of beans on toast for a weary walker. There was a string of outbuildings, one of which had its doors open. Inside were tables and chairs laid out in a manner that you might expect of a café. The furniture of stainless steel chairs and glass-topped tables felt sterile and the echoey tiled floor was cold. It appeared deserted. But it was out of the wind and represented a sanctuary. I began to empty my backpack, seeking my dry secondary set of evening garb: a thermal top and leggings, shorts, a tech-tee and my trail shoes. I had carried these clothes 241 miles from Fort William to where I was now, unused. I had begun to loath them as unnecessary baggage. Freeloading passengers along for the ride. At that moment I was grateful that I had carried them the distance. Everything had a purpose.

I had felt a sense of balance on this walk. I had been so lucky with the weather and more recently with the MOD, not to mention my windfall burger and chips in Kinlochewe. Events conspired to gently ease me along the way, nurturing me and giving me companionship and sustenance when needed, as if forces beyond my understanding, beyond my control, had been propelling me northwards. I am not superstitious. I do not believe in Gods and Goddesses. But at that moment, I couldn't help but wonder if there was a greater divinity out there casting half a smile my way.

Then Ange appeared, almost like magic, through the serving hatch in the café, not unlike the moustachioed fez-wearing fancy-dress shopkeeper in Mr Benn. Only without the moustache and fez, and more like an angelic apparition. She asked if I would like a cup of tea. I bluntly stated that I had just fallen in a bog up to my waist and did she have anywhere I could wash the worst of the slime off? Without batting an eyelid she climbed through the hatch into the café and gestured for me to follow her to the bathroom, explaining apologetically that there was no hot water.

A short time later I had changed and, warm and cosy, was in a much better state of mind. I regrouped back at the café. I retrieved a plastic bottle of golden liquid from my belongings. A very special liquid that I had carried with me from the beginning in anticipation of this moment. Twelve star Metaxa. Fine Greek brandy. A 50th birthday present from my brother-in-law, Martin. I was about to take a mouthful when Ange appeared once more. She asked if I would like a beer. This would have been manna from heaven if I'd been a beer drinker. I thanked her but declined, explaining that I had brought brandy with me. She then thoughtfully produced a heavy cut glass tumbler. After imbibing tea, soup, hot chocolate, wine and brandy from the same plastic camping mug, a cut glass tumbler represented great opulence. I thanked Ange again for her thoughtfulness and took a satisfying gulp of Metaxa. The warmth of the spirit reached parts of my body that thought they had been permanently ostracised, namely my toes.

After belated introductions and me apologising for my clumsy skills of communication, Ange explained she was John's daughter and had been living with him at the lighthouse for over a year. It was without doubt an isolated lifestyle and at times, mainly in the winter months, very difficult. However, the positives and beauty of Cape Wrath outweighed the hardships, she explained. After the past two weeks I completely understood and couldn't agree more. I even felt a pang of envy.

Ange asked if I would like a bed in their bunkroom. I gently mentioned that I was happy with sleeping under canvas and was averse to sharing a bedroom with others. She told me that as I was the only one there, I would have the place to myself, so I agreed to check out what was on offer. She led me through a maze of cluttered buildings stacked high with everything you wouldn't dream of throwing out if you were living on the edge of civilisation. My expectations were low when I entered the bunkroom and the smell of varnished wood hit me. The room was beautifully renovated. Polished Norwegian pine floorboards furnished with antique wrought iron bedsteads bedecked in pristine white duvets. I hastily reappraised my opinion and gratefully accepted the offer of sleeping in a real bed for the first time since leaving home.

Once I was settled, I headed back to the café where Ange offered to cook me dinner. I declined, as I had brought food with me. She seemed disappointed and settled for giving me the last huge piece of chocolate brownie, saying that it was on the house as she was going to make a new batch. She then left me to my own thoughts.

Not being accustomed to traditional solid buildings I felt a little claustrophobic and ventured outside. It was a stunning evening. I couldn't have imagined a more perfect ending to such an epic odyssey. I found a cliff top perch and gazed out to sea as the sun slowly sank towards the Atlantic horizon. Perfectly balanced with a chocolate brownie in one hand and a glass of Metaxa in the other, I felt happy. I tried to take in every detail of the moment, absorbing and holding on to all that I was feeling. The rawness and immersion of the past 13 days flowed through me. I wasn't euphoric. I didn't even feel relief at completing the task. I was over all that. What I felt was an overwhelming sense of contentment. I was exactly where I should be. I had achieved what I had set out to do. What I had dared not believe I was capable of. I had done it and done it well. The best I could have done. I did feel a tinge of melancholy that the adventure was over and that I would soon be leaving the Highlands. But all felt balanced and my heart was telling me it was time to head home to my family. I fumbled for my tracker and sent the pre-set "All good, I'm camping here for the night" message. I sent the message three times in succession as pre-arranged to signify that I had made it to my goal.

Again I felt tears running down my cheeks. I was enveloped in a feeling of utter contentedness that I have only ever felt in very rare special moments of my life. I was so happy, so lucky, so privileged to be where I was. Right there. Right then.

Total walked: 240.8 miles

Total ascent: 13,279 metres

Total raised for MIND: £1000

Sandwood Bay.

Red flags flying at the Cape Wrath bombing range.

The Cape Wrath lighthouse.

Cape Wrath Trail + 1

Cape Wrath lighthouse to Durness
Very few miles walked
Very few metres of ascent

After a good night's sleep, the kind of slumber you might have after walking 241 miles, I woke up refreshed but in something of a dreamlike state. Mentally I was still adjusting to the idea that there was no more walking to be done. It felt strange that I didn't have an objective, a place to walk to over 20 miles away. I did need to extricate myself from Cape Wrath, but all that would happen naturally with little effort from me. I had my familiar Ready Brek at 6am. I went for a stroll along the cliff tops and picked a place with a perfect view to dig my last hole for morning ablutions. I then returned to the bunkhouse to pack up.

I spent the next four hours scrawling notes. The previous evening I had made a conscious decision not to write anything. To just enjoy the moment. That morning my thoughts spilled from me. Flowing like a Highland mountain river in spate I covered the reverse of five sheets of my map squares in concise script. Part of the process was a cathartic exercise and the rest was a vain attempt to capture my feelings in that moment.

At some point Ange appeared at the café hatch and offered me a second breakfast, which I gratefully accepted and snaffled. She also presented me the lighthouse Cape Wrath Trail logbook. There were less than a dozen entries for 2019 and Ange explained that not all people who walk the Cape Wrath Trail choose to stop at the lighthouse. I read others' experiences, including a chap who had started in Edale, linking the Pennine Way to other national trails, walking through blizzards to finally finish in glorious sunshine. Another entry was surprisingly emotionless and dull, stating miles covered and conditions underfoot like some kind of financial report.

My entry read:

> *"What an amazing adventure. I feel privileged and humbled to have walked through the Highlands. I will look back on these past 13 days with profound happiness for the rest of my life. This part of the world will forever be in my heart.*
>
> *I cannot express enough gratitude to John and Ange here at the Ozone Café. Their kind and generous hospitality made a perfect end to a magical walk."*

Perhaps a little over the top but I felt compelled to redress the staid dispassionate summaries of some people's Cape Wrath Trail reports. I wondered if they had done the same walk I had.

Around mid-morning, Brian, who I had first met at the Rhiconich Hotel, turned up. Despite all his insider military connections he had misunderstood that it was

NOT safe to cross the active range. He was spotted by one of the MOD safety marshals around 9am. They picked him up and whisked him the remaining section of the way in their Land Rover. Fortunately for Brian, the Royal Air Force had decided that they were done for the weekend and had not carried out their morning sortie. The very nice MOD marshal offered us both a lift to where the ferry departed across the Kyle of Durness. In that way we were able to avoid the minibus that carried the day-trippers to and from the lighthouse. It also saved us five quid each. I was surprised at the respect and courtesy afforded to us as people who had travelled there on foot.

The marshal apologised because he had to drive a circuitous route around the Cape to take the red flags down. This was a bonus for me as I had my very own guide and got a tour of the peninsula. The chap explained that it was very rare for any bombs to actually be dropped onto the range. Occasionally the moorland was strafed by aircraft, and about a decade ago an itinerant shell blasted from a naval vessel almost destroyed the house where the marshals lived whilst on duty. It left a 300-metre gash in the landscape only a stone's throw from the cottage.

Amongst other places, we visited Kearvaig Bothy. This is quite possibly the most scenically located bothy in all of Scotland. And there is some serious competition for this accolade. Located in a truly isolated setting, it would take some perseverance to get to it, but you would be richly rewarded. Kearvaig Bothy even has its own stunning sandy beach.

Arriving at the slipway, our guide arranged for the ferry operator to make an unscheduled trip just for us. To be fair, the ferry operator was only too happy to make a few extra pounds whilst waiting for the day-trippers to return from the lighthouse. The ferry was a small open-top plastic molded boat with a 25-horsepower outboard engine on the back and a pair of scaffolding poles strapped to oval cut plywood for oars. I hoped the engine wouldn't fail. The tide was out, which probably meant there was half the distance to travel. I wasn't grumbling either way, as my luck continued to hold, and on reaching the far side of the bay I was offered a lift covering the last few miles from the harbour to Durness village.

I pitched up at the well-appointed campsite and plundered the facilities. It felt distinctly odd camping amongst others on well marked out plots. I showered and availed myself of the laundry facilities to rid my apparel and me of Scottish slime and my grime. I'm not sure which was worse, me or my clothes! The wind had picked up and the forecast was for snow so I made good use of the "campers' kitchen", a comparatively cosy outbuilding, which offered power points and wifi. I caught up on communications whilst sipping a glass of Merlot which I'd recently purloined from the Durness Spar. The campsite bar and restaurant supplied further sustenance before I retired.

Snow on the hills the day after completing the walk.

Cape Wrath Trail + 2

Durness to Kinlochbervie to Dundonnell
Many miles by bus and car

I snaffled a bacon butty at the campsite before catching the local bus back to Kinlochbervie where I hoped to meet David, my brother-in-law. The bus driver kindly dropped me off at Old School House café where I had enjoyed a Scottish breakfast only two days before, although with time feeling elastic it felt as though it had been an age, or possibly a lifetime, since I had previously visited. The proprietor recognised me and welcomed me like an old friend. I enjoyed my second, or possibly my third, breakfast of the day. Clearly my body had missed the memo that walking had now finished and no more calories were needed. Or maybe it knew something I didn't, because just outside snow was flurrying. Mr Snow Flake and all his friends had come out to play.

Just for old times' sake, and because I had agreed to meet David at the Spar in Kinlochbervie, I re-walked the 4 miles down the road to the village. Only this time it was through intermittent blizzards. Still a little ahead of the allotted meeting time, I checked into another café for a tea and met Rowena who I had last seen well over a week ago at

Maol Bhuidhe Bothy. It took us both a moment or two to place each other. I was able to assure her that the bombing range was safe to cross and wished her good luck.

After drinking my tea and having read all the local literature that the café had to offer (twice) I paid up and left to call David. I was fumbling for my phone in the car park outside the café when a vaguely familiar white vehicle pulled in with a very familiar driver. Serendipity continued to weave its magic.

It was a wonderful and slightly surreal reunion. I'm not entirely sure what David expected, but to me he represented a physical and solid connection to my recent, but also recently distant, world. It didn't take long to reconnect and for me to find firm anchorage.

And that is pretty much the end of my Cape Wrath Trail odyssey. David safely delivered me home three days later by which time my feet had more or less totally recovered.

TWO WEEKS LATER

Typing this several weeks later the whole thing feels like a fading dream. Almost as if it had been someone else who had done the walk. I look back at the photos with something approaching amazement that it was me in that scenery and apparently I walked 241 miles. I still don't feel like a particularly gnarly outdoor type but I am pleased I can continue to surprise and even confound my greatest critic... me.

The next challenge? The gremlins in me vie for attention. I've learned that they cannot be trusted. They will take me to the edge of reason and then shake my hand as I topple into oblivion. I have had a small glimpse of what drives people to climb mountains and walk to the poles. I still hear the sirens call but for me, at least for now, there are nobler challenges to distract me, this time with my family. A(nother) van trip is afoot. A year of exploration and discovery. New countries. New people. New adventures. No doubt it will be a voyage into the unknown. Both inwards and outwards…

How hard can it be? What could possibly go wrong?

ABOUT THE AUTHOR

Will Cove lives with his long-suffering wife, two daughters and two cats on the northern fringes of the Peak District. When not traipsing around the countryside, he sometimes works as a graphic designer. His passions include travel, paragliding and cooking. He has even been known to combine all three, bundling his family into a small camper van and heading off to explore Europe and a little further afield for a year. Not once but twice.

He generally lives by the mantras of "How hard can it be?" and "What could possibly go wrong?" Even he has to admit, though, that sometimes living by these mantras doesn't work out for the best. When his adages fail him, his unusually well-developed streak of stubbornness to survive has pulled him through the various life-limiting situations he has found himself in. This strategy has always worked for him... so far.

OTHER BOOKS BY WILL COVE

A couple of years before he embarked on the Southern Upland Way, Will Cove successfully completed his first ever long distance walk, Wainwright's Coast to Coast. He just about got from St Bees to Robin Hood's Bay unscathed. By luck more than judgement. With that single victory he thought he knew everything there was to know about walking a long way.

The Southern Upland Way is a coast-to-coast route through southern Scotland, but one which is much less trodden, even by those walkers who have followed in Alfred Wainwright's English coast-to-coast footsteps. There are fewer places to stay. Fewer shops. And most of all, fewer pubs. But where's the adventure if there is no jeopardy? How hard can it be? What could possibly go wrong?

Buoyed by the naive confidence of someone who has no idea of just how much they are lacking in experience, Will gamely bid his family farewell at Portpatrick, on the west coast, and started walking east. Logic suggested the prevailing winds would be on his back, gently helping him each step of the way.

Little did he know that he would spend most of the next two weeks walking into the teeth of the Beast from the East. Through ferocious winds, sideways rain and blizzards. More of an ordeal by ice than a baptism by fire.

This is the account of one fool's stubborn ability to keep going when the conditions strongly suggested he should run away. And how, through adversity, he discovered unexpected shelter, new friendship and hidden treasure.

Whilst this account is by no means a step-by-step guide to walking the Southern Upland Way, if you are toying with the idea of this long distance route, or even if you are just a little curious about what is involved, then you could do worse than learn from the lessons endured by Will and be entertained by his blunders from the comfort of your warm and comfortable living room.

THERE & BACK
AGAIN... *almost*

*A Pennine Way walk –
400 miles up and down
the spine of England,
wild camping (nearly)
all the way*

Will Cove

When Will Cove first thought about walking the Pennine Way, being a seasoned walker, he didn't think it would be too taxing. He initially thought he'd walk north to south so he'd be finishing near his home on the northern fringes of the Peak District. He thought he'd enjoy a few convivial pub stops and maybe a cosy night or two at a B&B. But that was before the coronavirus pandemic hit.

In April 2021, as the third lockdown ended, pubs, restaurants and cafes were beginning to open up again, but they were restricted to serving food and drinks outside. Hotels, B&Bs and campsites were still closed. Even Scotland, where Will had planned to start the Pennine

Way, was closed. If he was going to walk the Pennine Way anytime soon, his plans would need to be flexible.

When he set off from Edale, now walking the traditional direction south to north, he hoped Scotland would be open by the time he arrived. He hoped his family would meet him at the finish. He hoped for sun, not snow. As he began the long, slow climb up onto the Kinder Scout plateau, he couldn't help noticing how much his plans were based on hope.

This is the account of how one person unwittingly managed to walk to Kirk Yetholm, the end of the Pennine Way, and then decided to turn around and walk back again... almost.

The Vagabond and the Pilgrim

Walking over 1,000 miles from the most southerly point to the most northerly point of mainland Britain, wild camping most of the way.

Will Cove

Whilst walking the Pennine Way, Will Cove bumped into a fellow long distance walker who told him of people who chose to walk all the way from one end of Britain to the other. When he first heard about the concept of walking over a thousand miles in one go, the idea struck him as complete madness. At best it was the embodiment of British eccentricity; at worst it was self-indulgent folly. He swiftly dismissed the idea and forgot all about it.

Several months after arriving at Kirk Yetholm, the end of the Pennine Way, and then deciding to turn around and walk back again (that's another story, and a different book), Will realised he had been putting one foot in front of the other since he was two years old. How hard could it be to walk another thousand miles?

Will decided to wild camp as he went. This was partly because he had no idea how far he would be able to walk each day and partly because warm dry pubs, B&Bs and hotels were beyond his frugal ethos. And truth be told, it was mainly because he enjoyed being embedded in nature.

This is the story of how Will became both a vagabond and a pilgrim as he walked over a thousand miles from the most southerly point to the most northerly point of mainland Britain.

Printed in Dunstable, United Kingdom

77122413R00100

THINGS THAT
DISAPPEAR

ALSO BY JENNY ERPENBECK

The Book of Words
The End of Days
Go, Went, Gone
Kairos
Not a Novel
The Old Child and Other Stories
Visitation

THINGS THAT DISAPPEAR

JENNY ERPENBECK

translated from the German by Kurt Beals

GRANTA

Granta Publications, 12 Addison Avenue, London W11 4QR

First published in Great Britain by Granta Books in 2025

First published in the United States by New Directions, New York, in 2025
First published in the original German as *Dinge, die verschwinden* by Galiani Verlag, Berlin,
an imprint of Verlag Kiepenheuer & Witsch, in 2009

Copyright © 2009 by Verlag Kiepenheuer & Witsch GmbH & Co.
Translation copyright © 2025 by Kurt Beals

The translation of this work was supported by a grant from the
Goethe-Institut, which is funded by the German Ministry of Foreign Affairs.

Some of these pieces previously appeared in *Urbainable/Stadthaltig* (Akademie der Künste),
Heat, *The Paris Review*, *The Point*, *The Threepenny Review*, and *The Yale Review*

The poem on p. 96 appears in *The Gallows Songs: Christian Morgenstern's "Galgenlieder,"*
translated by Max Knight (University of California Press, 1966).
Used by permission of Insel Verlag.

A CIP catalogue record for this book is available from the British Library.

1 3 5 7 9 10 8 6 4 2

ISBN 978 1 80351 299 0
eISBN 978 1 80351 300 3

Typeset in Adobe Garamond Pro by Iram Allam

Printed and bound by CPI Group (UK) Ltd, Croydon, CR0 4YY

The manufacturer's authorised representative in the EU for product safety is
Authorised Rep Compliance Ltd, 71 Lower Baggot Street,
Dublin D02 P593, Ireland. www.arccompliance.com

www.granta.com